IN SEARCH OF THE CORE OF CORE COMPETENCIES

A STUDY INVESTIGATING THEORETICAL FOUNDATIONS, DEFINITIONS, ORGANIZATIONAL IMPLICATIONS, AND ANALYSIS METHODOLOGIES

Mark Vos

In Search of the Core of Core Competencies
1993 Dutch original by Mark Vos
2026 English translation by Mark Vos

ISBN: 979-8-234-06844-6

TABLE OF CONTENTS

Table of Contents 3

Foreword 7

Preface 11

Summary 13

Introduction 19

Chapter 1: Core Competencies & Co. 25

§ 1.1 The Core Competence Concept and its Positioning 25

§ 1.1.1 The Core Competence Concept..26

§ 1.1.2 Positioning in Time 27

§ 1.1.3 Positioning According to Paradigms 29

§ 1.2 Orthodox Economic Theories 32

§ 1.2.1 Marshall..33

§ 1.2.2 Coase 34

§ 1.2.3 Williamson 35

§ 1.3 Concepts for the Strategic Leadership Phase 36

§ 1.3.1 Drivers..36

§ 1.3.2 Invisible Assets..39

§ 1.3.3 Resource-based Analysis..42

§ 1.3.4 Core Competencies 44

§ 1.3.5 Core Capabilities 47

§ 1.4 Preliminary Conclusions 50

§ 1.4.1 A Different Perspective on the Firm 50

§ 1.4.2 What Are Differences With Legacy Concepts? 51

Chapter 2: Intellectual Roots 55

§ 2.1 Criticism of Orthodox Economic Theories 55

§ 2.2 Foundational Pillars of the Core Competence Concept 57

§ 2.2.1 The Schumpeterian Firm and Environment 58

§ 2.2.2 Penrose's Learning Theory of the Firm 61

§ 2.2.3 The Organizational Routines of Nelson & Winter 64
§ 2.3 Characteristics of the Core Competence Concept 68
§ 2.3.1 Organizational Learning 68
§ 2.3.2 Path Dependencies 71
§ 2.3.3 Selection-Environment 73
§ 2.4 Conclusion 75

Chapter 3: A Closer Examination of Competence 77
§ 3.1 The Components of a Core Competence 77
§ 3.1.1 Synthesis: Core Competence, Resource-Based View, and Core Capability 77
§ 3.1.2 Knowledge Base 80
§ 3.1.3 Customer Value 81
§ 3.1.4 Managerial Capabilities 82
§ 3.2 Defining Core Competence 83
§ 3.2.1 Interaction Knowledge Base – Managerial Capabilities 84
§ 3.2.2 Interaction Knowledge Base – Customer Value 85
§ 3.2.3 Interaction Managerial Capabilities – Customer Value 85
§ 3.2.4 Intersection of the Three Components: Core Competence .86
§ 3.3 Stages of Competence 90
§ 3.3.1 No Competence in a Component....................................92
§ 3.3.2 Competence in Non-Overlapping Components 92
§ 3.3.3 Competence in Overlapping Components........................93
§ 3.3.4 Core Competence 94
§ 3.4 Analysis of a Firm's Core Competencies..........................95
§ 3.4.1 Level of Analysis: End Products 96
§ 3.4.2 Level of Analysis: Business Processes............................96
§ 3.4.3 Level of Analysis: Corporate and SBU Levels 97
§ 3.4.4 Level of Analysis: Benchmarking 97
§ 3.4.5 Integration of the Levels of Analysis 98
§ 3.5 Conclusion..99

Chapter 4: Organizational Implications 101
§ 4.1 Approaches to Organizations 101

§ 4.1.1 Streams Within the Organizational Literature...............101

§ 4.1.2 Cybernetic and Holographic Organizing Principles..........104

§ 4.2 Holography and Core Competence 109

§ 4.2.1 Redundancy of Functions and Core Competence 110

§ 4.2.2 Requisite Variety and Core Competence 111

§ 4.2.3 Minimum Critical Specification and Core Competence ...111

§ 4.2.4 Learning to Learn and Core Competence........................112

§ 4.3 Holographic Principles in Sector and Country Processes 113

§ 4.3.1 Best: The New Competition 114

§ 4.3.2 Application of Best to Core Competence Management....116

§ 4.3.3 Porter: The Diamond 118

§ 4.3.4 Application of Porter to Core Competence Management .118

§ 4.4 Conclusion..121

Chapter 5: Tradition Revisited 123

§ 5.1 From *Experience Curve* to *Competence Curve* 123

§ 5.1.1 The *Experience Curve* 124

§ 5.1.2 The *Competence Curve* 125

§ 5.2 From *Product Portfolio* to *Competence Portfolio*.............127

§ 5.2.1 The *Product Portfolio* 127

§ 5.2.2 The *Competence Portfolio*......................................130

§ 5.3 From *Diversification Strategies* to *Competence Strategies* .132

§ 5.3.1 *Diversification Strategies* 132

§ 5.3.2 *Competence Strategies* 133

§ 5.4 From *Value Chain* to *Competence Chain*......................135

§ 5.4.1 The *Value Chain* 135

§ 5.4.2 The *Competence Chain* 137

§ 5.5 Conclusion...140

Chapter 6: Conclusion 141

§ 6.1 Theoretical Contribution Vis-à-Vis Existing Literature.......141

§ 6.1.1 Comparative Assessment: Core Competence....................141

§ 6.1.2 Comparative Assessment: Core Capabilities 144

§ 6.2 Empirical Relevance and Practical Application...................145

§ 6.2.1 Comparative Assessment: Resource-Based Analysis 146

§ 6.2.2 Comparative Analysis: Nedlloyd's Audit 149

§ 6.3 Critiques of the Core Competence Concept 152

§ 6.4 Evaluation of Research Objectives and Future Directions... 154

§ 6.4.1 Review of Objectives 155

§ 6.4.2 Directions for Future Research.. 156

§ 6.4.3 Concluding remarks 158

Appendix A **161**

Appendix B... **171**

Appendix C **173**

Appendix D **179**

Bibliography **185**

FOREWORD

This book began its life as a Master's thesis in Business Administration at Erasmus University Rotterdam in 1993. At that time, the concept of core competence was already a powerful lens through which to understand why some firms create enduring value while others, despite resources and ambition, struggle to sustain advantage. The original study asked a deceptively simple question: what is the core of core competencies? That question led into a broader investigation of theoretical foundations, definitions, organizational implications, and methods of analysis. More than three decades later, that question remains important. In fact, in an era shaped by artificial intelligence, rapidly shifting markets, and strategic uncertainty, it may be more relevant than ever.

The decision to publish the thesis in English is not only an act of translation, but also of recontextualization. The business world of 1993 was already changing, yet the pace and scope of change now confronting firms is of a different order. AI is not merely another productivity tool. It affects the cognitive foundations of work itself: analysis, drafting, decision support, pattern recognition, coordination, and even the generation of content, code, and recommendations. Previous waves of automation transformed physical labor and standardized industrial processes. This wave reaches into the core of knowledge work. For that reason, many firms are not simply adapting; they are being forced to rethink what business they are truly in.

Across industries, the pattern is becoming increasingly visible. In transportation, the gig economy model that disrupted traditional taxi services now faces the next disruption through autonomy. Uber once changed the logic of urban mobility; AI may in turn challenge Uber's own position by changing the very economics of dispatch, routing, and vehicle operation. In retail, the shift from e-commerce toward AI-optimized commerce is already underway, where algorithms increasingly shape assortment, pricing, merchandising, and personalization. The store is no longer just a physical or digital location; it is becoming a decision system. In media and entertainment, generative tools are moving the industry from scarcity to abundance, changing not only production but also the role of the creator. In software development, AI agents are transforming the developer's role from direct builder to supervisor, orchestrator, and integrator of increasingly self-building systems. Logistics is moving from optimization to orchestration, finance from digitization to autonomous decision-making, healthcare from digitization to AI-augmented judgment, legal services from document handling to AI-supported legal reasoning, and education from online content delivery to personalized tutoring at massive scale.

These examples matter because they show that AI is not simply improving existing processes. It is altering the structure of value creation in many sectors. In that environment, firms cannot rely on incremental efficiency alone. They need a more fundamental strategic anchor. That anchor is core competence.

Core competence thinking remains compelling because it directs attention to what a firm can do better than others, what it can do in a way that is difficult to imitate, and what it can continually develop as conditions change. When the foundations of industries are being reshaped, identifying, nurturing, and extending core competencies becomes more than a strategic exercise. It becomes a blueprint for survival and for growth. Schumpeter's notion of creative destruction is not an abstract historical idea in this moment; it is visible in daily business decisions, in startup formation, in the acceleration of platform power, and in the pressure placed on established firms to reinvent themselves before the market does it for them.

This book is also significant because it sought early on to connect the core competence concept with its managerial and organizational implications. In doing so, it anticipated later developments in the dynamic capabilities literature, which emphasized the firm's ability to adapt competencies in changing environments. In hindsight, the thesis can be seen as part of a broader intellectual transition: from seeing competence as a relatively stable asset to understanding it as something living, cumulative, and adaptive. A firm's advantage does not reside only in what it knows, but in how it learns, how it organizes, and how it converts knowledge into customer value over time.

A central contribution of this study is its incorporation of holographic organizing and learning principles as managerial capabilities of the firm. This perspective rests on the idea that core competence is not a single trait or isolated resource, but an interdependent system. It comprises three essential elements. First, there is the firm's knowledge base: the collective memory of the organization, including routines, know-how, and accumulated experience. Second, there is the delivery of customer value: competencies only matter when they create value in practice, and that value creation also generates learning opportunities. Third, there are the managerial capabilities that make competence growth possible: the ability to expand the knowledge base, maintain focus on value delivery, and create the conditions for learning and coordination. A core competence emerges when these three elements reinforce one another and are aligned.

That insight remains highly relevant today. In a turbulent environment, companies often make the mistake of reacting to change by scattering attention across too many initiatives. They chase trends, imitate competitors, or pursue AI for its own sake. Yet AI should not be adopted as a vague symbol of progress. It should be used with strategic clarity. The important question is not whether a firm uses AI, but whether AI strengthens the competencies that matter most to its future. Does it deepen the knowledge base? Does it improve the delivery of customer value? Does it enhance learning, coordination, and judgment? If the answer is yes, then AI becomes a force multiplier rather than a distraction.

The original thesis also recognized that more work remains to be done in building tools and methods that help CEOs and boards steer organizations with confidence. That remains true, perhaps even more urgently than before. Leaders today face volatile markets, technological discontinuity, shifting customer expectations, and pressure from new competitors that are often born AI-native. Under such conditions, strategic language alone is not enough. Boards and executives need practical ways to identify which competencies are truly core, how those competencies can be measured and developed, and how they can be protected while still allowing the firm to evolve.

This book therefore speaks both to continuity and change. Its central argument has endured: firms need a clear understanding of what makes them distinctive and how that distinctiveness is created, maintained, and renewed. But its relevance has also intensified because the contemporary business environment is changing at a speed that makes strategic drift more dangerous than ever. The purpose of republishing this work is to offer readers not just a historical document, but a living framework for thinking about the future.

The turbulence surrounding us should not obscure the strategic opportunity it contains. AI is a threat to complacency, to undifferentiated business models, and to organizations that mistake automation for strategy. But AI is also an extraordinary opportunity to strengthen core competencies, deepen distinctive capabilities, and amplify competitive advantage. In that sense, the present moment does not weaken the case for core competence thinking; it makes it indispensable. In an age of uncertainty, steady focus on its core competencies may be the most important source of direction a firm can have.

Mark Vos
Los Angeles, April 2026

PREFACE

This thesis is submitted in partial fulfillment of the requirements for the degree of Master's of Science in Business Administration at the Erasmus University Rotterdam. This thesis presents a theoretical examination of the core competence concept and related theories. In the preparation of this thesis, I am indebted to several individuals for their contributions.

Primarily, I extend my gratitude to my advisor, Prof. dr. ir. van den Bosch, and my readers, Prof. dr. van Berkel and Prof. dr. drs. Janszen. Their constructive criticism and valuable insights significantly enhanced the content during the development of this work.

Furthermore, I express my appreciation to drs. van der Zaal for his sustained interest and support of this research, which positively influenced the trajectory of this thesis. I am indebted to drs. Biemans and N. Verlage for numerous stimulating discussions on this subject, their constructive critique, and for a brilliant time during my studies.

To refine the conceptual framework of this study, a series of interviews was conducted with practitioners actively engaged with the core competence concept. I gratefully acknowledge the time and cooperation extended by the following individuals: drs. Vossenaar (Nedlloyd), drs. Kiewit (Nedlloyd), M. Raida (The Boston Consulting Group), M.P. Eikelenboom (The Boston Consulting Group), and Prof. ir. Dinklo (Philips). Additionally, I thank N. Verlage and G. Oberdorf for the provision of essential computer resources.

Finally, I offer my deepest thanks to my parents. Their unwavering support and understanding provided the foundation necessary for me to pursue my academic and personal goals during my studies.

Each of these individuals has contributed uniquely to the research presented herein. Any assumptions, assertions, and mistakes are my own.

Rotterdam, June 1993

SUMMARY

In recent years, several concepts have emerged that position a firm's capabilities as the foundation for strategic decision-making. Adopting an *inside-out* perspective on the firm, these frameworks are collectively designated herein as *core competence concepts*.

The emergence of these concepts is a response to traditional strategic frameworks reaching their functional limits, a saturation driven by the escalating demands of the corporate environment. As the business landscape has become increasingly turbulent and complex, strategic concepts have necessarily evolved. Core competence concepts are situated within the most recent developmental phase, the *Strategic Leadership* phase (Henzler 1988). Paradigmatically, these concepts are rooted in the resource-based view of the firm. The dynamic capabilities paradigm expands upon this foundation, placing heightened emphasis on the continuous refinement and augmentation of firm-specific capabilities. The concepts of *drivers* (Porter 1991) and *invisible assets* (Itami 1987) serve as transitional mechanisms between the *resource-based view* and *dynamic capabilities* paradigms. Conversely, *resource-based view* (Collis 1991), *core competence* (Prahalad & Hamel 1990), and *core capability* (Stalk et al. 1992) are squarely situated within the dynamic capabilities paradigm.

These core competence concepts do not derive from the orthodox economic (equilibrium) theories associated with Marshall and his successors. Orthodox theories prioritize equilibrium, thereby neglecting structural economic and technological shifts—factors that are, in fact, primary drivers of environmental turbulence and complexity. Furthermore, a central pillar of orthodox theory is behavioral maximization, comprising three components: a general objective, a well-defined choice set, and rational choice. While the general objective is typically profit maximization, multiple—and potentially conflicting—objectives may exist. Moreover, the constraints of bounded rationality preclude the comprehensive evaluation of all possible choices. Consequently, orthodox theory treats firms as "black boxes" that respond identically to external stimuli. In contrast, core competence theory identifies inter-firm differences between firms as the source of competitive advantage, utilizing these differences as the unit of analysis. Thus, core competence theory cannot locate its theoretical foundations within orthodox economics. Conversely, theoretical foundations are identified in the works of Schumpeter (1987), Penrose (1972), and Nelson & Winter (1982).

Schumpeter explicitly accounts for structural environmental changes, arguing innovation as the engine of the capitalist market economy. The entrepreneur occupies a pivotal role, seeking novel possibilities in products, design, production processes, and organizational forms. To realize this *implementation of new combinations*, the firm must adopt a dynamic organizational structure.

Penrose expands upon this via the concept of *productive services*, arguing that resources per se are not production inputs; rather, the inputs are the services those resources yield. It is this service difference between firms that renders each firm unique. Firm growth is driven by the release of managerial services, which function to integrate entrepreneurial services into the existing administrative architecture. Upon the successful execution of this integration, a theoretical surplus of managerial services is generated, creating an incentive for further expansion. As Penrose (1972:137) notes: *"In the long run the profitability, survival and growth of a firm does not depend so much on the efficiency with which it is able to organize the production of even a widely diversified range of products as it does on the ability of the firm to establish one or more wide and relatively impregnable 'bases' from which it can adapt and extend its operations in an uncertain, changing, and competitive world."*

Nelson & Winter introduce the concept of *organizational routines*, which function analogously to individual capabilities. Organizational members possess sets of routines (*repertoires*) selectable for specific activities. These organizational routines form the firm's memory: *"...organizations remember by doing"* (Nelson & Winter 1982:99). Significantly, these routines are not antithetical to innovation; they are subject to improvement, and novel combinations of routines can drive innovation (*implementation of new combinations*). Indeed, the innovation process is itself a routine. While the outcome of innovation is uncertain, the trajectory of the search process typically adheres to established routines and patterns

These three theories form the intellectual lineage of the core competence concept. Drawing from these foundations, three distinct characteristics of the concept can be identified. The first is organizational learning, which facilitates acquiring new knowledge and experience, thereby enabling continued firm growth. Learning occurs in two ways: adaptive (single-loop) and generative (double-loop). Adaptive learning drives improvement within the parameters of existing norms, whereas generative learning examines the underlying norms themselves, enabling the development of entirely new routines.

The second characteristic is *path dependency*. A primary consequence of the inside-out perspective is that the firm's current configuration exerts a profound influence on its available strategic options. Since the firm evolves from its existing activities, its learning trajectory is constrained by its history.

The third characteristic pertains to the firm's *selection-environment*, which may be stratified into three distinct resource cycles. In the *slow-resource cycle*, competitive advantage can be sustained for relatively long durations. In the *standard-resource cycle*, sustainability becomes more difficult, while in the *fast-resource cycle*, such possibilities are severely curtailed due to the idea-driven (Schumpeterian) nature of competition. Consequently, the need for core competence thinking intensifies as the resource cycle shortens.

This study synthesizes these intellectual roots with the core competence framework and delineates the interdependent components of a core competence: *Knowledge Base*, *Customer Value*, and *Managerial Capabilities*. The Knowledge Base serves as the organizational memory, housing all knowledge and experience, both explicit and tacit. It is the locus of adaptive learning and, in conjunction with Managerial Capabilities, facilitates the generative learning required to expand the base. Customer Value represents the utility provided to the customer; it is defined not in monetary terms, but by the functionality that satisfies a specific need. Through Customer Value, the firm differentiates itself in the marketplace. Managerial Capabilities represent the capacity to align the Knowledge Base with Customer Value. Key elements of this capacity include the *Implementation of new combinations*, the coordination of routines, generative learning, and the execution of managerial roles such as *designer*, *teacher*, and *steward*.

Knowledge Vase, Customer Value, and Managerial Capabilities constitute the three primary components of a core competence. Through the complex interactions among them, a core competence is defined as the nexus of these three elements. Distinct stages of competence maturity can be identified: the absence of competence in any single component, competence within a single component, competence arising from interactions between components, and finally, the coming together of all three (the core competence). At this intersection, this core, continuous interaction ensures the perpetual alignment of the components. These stages correlate with the evolutionary trajectory of an industry (the selection-environment). In certain industries, competitiveness may be sustained via a single component; in others, it requires the interaction of components; ultimately, some industries demand the possession of fully integrated core competencies. It is argued that industrial evolution adheres to this developmental pattern.

Determining a firm's (core) competencies requires a multi-level analysis. The analysis of end products yields data regarding delivered Customer Value, as a direct link must exist between products and the needs they satisfy. At the corporate and Strategic Business Unit (SBU) levels, the focus shifts to identifying infrastructure that is conducive to competence development, thereby providing insight into Managerial Capabilities. An analysis of business processes—specifically the concepts underpinning them—offers a window into the firm's organizational routines and, by extension, its Knowledge Base. Subsequently, benchmarking serves to evaluate the firm's position relative to its competitors, given that competencies must be inherently distinctive or superior.

Regarding the organizational implications of the core competence concept, the most salient alignment is found within systems theory, specifically through cybernetic and holographic organizing principles. This framework yields four distinct principles: *redundancy of functions*, *requisite variety*, *minimum critical specification*, and *learning to learn*. The principle of redundancy of functions dictates that variety be embedded within functions to foster both generalization and specialization, thereby enhancing flexibility. The degree of variety required is governed by the principle of requisite variety, which asserts that variety must be introduced precisely where it is necessary; indeed, only internal variety can absorb external variety. Together, these principles create a self-organizing capacity within the system. To ensure this capacity evolves coherently, the remaining two principles are essential. The principle of minimum critical specification argues that management should function primarily as a facilitator, establishing the conditions that allow the system to self-structure. Finally, to mitigate the potential for chaos, the principle of learning to learn (analogous to generative learning) is paramount, ensuring the continuous development of a coherent normative framework for reference.

These organizational principles correlate with the components of a core competence, manifesting specifically in the integration of Customer Value into the repertoires of organizational members, the strategic introduction of variety across different levels of core competence components where utilized, and the facilitative function of Managerial Capabilities. Best and Porter have documented analogous processes at the sectoral and national levels, respectively.

Several strategic concepts were analyzed to assess their applicability within the core competence framework: the *experience curve, product portfolio, diversification strategies*, and the *value chain*. The experience curve is reconceptualized as a *competence curve*, demonstrating the positive correlation between "Cumulative delivered customer value" and the "Expansion of knowledge and experience within the Knowledge Base". The product portfolio is adapted into a *competence portfolio*, utilizing the variables of "Relative market share in functionality" and the "Improvement potential" of a competence; this model facilitates resource allocation across different core competencies. Diversification strategies are transformed into *competence strategies*, defined by the juxtaposition of core/non-core "Business" and core/non-core "Competence", thereby illustrating various growth trajectories based on the firm's core competencies. Finally, a novel application of the value chain is proposed. By relating value-creating activities to delivered Customer Value and analyzing them at the corporate level, activities can be grouped according to (core) competencies. This yields distinct *competence chains*, allowing for the identification of deficits in competencies or component interactions.

The principal contribution of this research, in relation to existing core competence frameworks, consists in the establishment of a robust theoretical foundation, the adoption of a comprehensive approach to the problem domain, and the identification of organizational implications. Consequently, this study significantly transcends prior efforts. The research methodology employed herein is advocated for the development of future core competence variants. This approach facilitates the examination of how such variants are positioned, their foundational pillars, their contribution to the definition, their organizational implications, and their relationship to existing concepts.

INTRODUCTION

In 1990, Prahalad and Hamel published their seminal article in the Harvard Business Review titled *"The Core Competence of the Corporation"*. The propositions advanced in this work were not entirely novel but represented a significant evolution within the resource-based view of the firm—a theoretical lineage established in the 1960s that had received scant attention in subsequent decades (Teece et al. 1990:2). The publication further built on the resource-based perspective, catalyzing considerable interest within strategic management discourse. This shift was evidenced not only by the proliferation of literature on the theme but also by the practical adoption of these concepts by firms. Fundamentally, a core competence is defined as a unique capability of a firm. Consequently, organizations should leverage these unique capabilities as the foundation for strategic decision-making. To secure and sustain competitive advantage, these capabilities must be continually cultivated and expanded.

In attempting to operationalize this concept, immediate limitations were encountered regarding the formulation presented by Prahalad and Hamel. Primarily, issues arose concerning the concept's applicability; it is defined with such ambiguity that practical implementation is rendered nearly impossible. The definition of a core competence is framed in broad terms, presenting significant challenges for empirical application. Furthermore, the lack of a rigorous methodology for identifying a firm's core competencies makes the process akin to a difficult, unstructured search. Second, the concept appears to lack a robust theoretical foundation. The article is written for a general audience, and the absence of theoretical grounding—or references thereto—is considered a significant deficiency. However, this study maintains that the foundational premises of the concept are of critical importance and that the aforementioned limitations can be effectively addressed.

Subsequent discussions with firms engaged in this area revealed two primary challenges concerning the core competence concept. First is the definition itself: there is significant ambiguity regarding the precise nature of a core competence, its functional mechanisms, and the methodology for its identification. The second area of uncertainty pertains to the organizational implications of the concept. Specifically, how should a firm structure itself around its core competencies? This issue has received negligible attention in the existing literature, a gap that inevitably prompts inquiry during implementation. A further question arises regarding how the core competence framework aligns with established strategic constructs, such as the product portfolio and the value chain. It remains to be determined whether these traditional concepts retain their relevance within the core competence paradigm.

This study aims to address these inquiries. Since "core competence" functions as a label for a specific construct—and analogous concepts have been developed under variant terminology—the term "core competence concept" is employed here to encompass these related theories. References to specific iterations of the concept will utilize their original nomenclature.

The problem statement and research objectives are formulated as follows:

1. Identification of the intellectual roots—specifically, the underlying theories—of the core competence concept, thereby providing a theoretical foundation for the core competence concept.
2. Drawing upon these theories to define core competence and describe its functional dynamics. The objective is to move beyond current theoretical limitations by operationalizing the concept and developing an analytical methodology for the identification of core competencies.
3. Delineation of the potential implications for organizing core competencies. Given the limited literature on this topic, this study proposes a conceptual framework for core competence management.
4. Assessment of the relationship between the core competence concept and existing strategic constructs to determine their applicability or amenability to adaptation.

The study is organized as follows. To explain the precise nature of the core competence concept and its place within the literature, Chapter One provides a comprehensive introduction. The concept is contextualized chronologically, acknowledging its rise to prominence only within the last three years. Furthermore, because the core competence concept rests on foundational premises different from other strategic approaches (such as game theory and the competitive forces model), it is situated across distinct theoretical paradigms. To explain the distinctions between traditional strategic concepts and the core competence approach, the origins of the former—rooted in orthodox economic theory—are briefly examined. The chapter concludes with an overview of the implications these differences hold for strategic decision-making.

In Chapter Two, grounded in a critique of the assumptions underlying orthodox economic theory, an exploration of alternative economic frameworks is undertaken. These alternatives include the macroeconomic theory of Schumpeter (1987), the meso-evolutionary theory of Nelson & Winter (1982), and the micro theory of the firm by Penrose (1972). It is argued that the intellectual roots of the core competence concept reside within these theories. Building on these frameworks, several characteristics of the core competence concept—specifically those relating to organizational learning, path dependencies, and the selection-environment—are examined. Through this analysis, the first research objective is addressed.

Chapter Three addresses the second objective. Synthesizing existing core competence concepts with their intellectual roots, a model of core competence is developed. This model identifies three core components: *Knowledge Base*, *Customer Value*, and *Managerial Capabilities*. This framework allows for the description of interaction processes that govern the emergence or absence of a core competence. The definition is thus operationalized within a model where functional dynamics are integral to the definition itself. Furthermore, the model is particularly effective for distinguishing between different stages of competence maturity. These competence stages are correlated with industry evolution—the selection-environment of the firm. The core competence concept further serves as the foundation for developing an analytical methodology for determining (core) competencies. Rather than functioning as a prescriptive checklist, this methodology outlines the criteria by which competencies may be assessed. It serves as a conceptual framework and guideline for identifying organizational competencies.

IN SEARCH OF THE CORE OF CORE COMPETENCIES

In alignment with the third objective, Chapter Four addresses the potential organizational implications of the core competence concept. Rather than compiling a disparate list of relevant points from various organizational theories, a single model is adopted, grounded in the cybernetic and holographic organizing principles formulated by Morgan (1986). These principles are integrated with the core competence model developed in Chapter Three to establish a comprehensive framework. To substantiate the described organizing processes, the analysis draws upon the work of Best (1990) and Porter (1990). Both authors delineate analogous processes at the sectoral and national levels, respectively, thereby providing a deeper understanding of the organizing processes discussed. This model also serves as the conceptual framework for core competence management.

Chapter Five addresses the inquiries related to the fourth objective. Here, four traditional strategic concepts are critically examined: the *experience curve, product portfolio, diversification strategies,* and the *value chain.* Each concept is analyzed to determine the significance of its core variables and the differentiating capabilities they generate, which in turn yield specific insights. The function of these variables is then mapped to their potential role within the core competence concept, or their substitution by alternative variables. While the intent is not to supplant these traditional concepts, it is argued that the models adapted within the core competence framework offer superior insight compared to their original formulations.

The study concludes in Chapter Six by outlining the value added by this research. While this assessment is inherently selective, every effort is made to provide robust substantiation. The added value is determined through a comparison with existing core competence models, a case study of the ball bearing industry, and the core competence analysis process at Nedlloyd. Finally, critiques of the core competence concept are addressed, and priorities for future research are identified.

This study aims to transcend existing concepts within the field. Beyond positioning the concept and uncovering its intellectual roots, an attempt is made to define core competence and describe its functional dynamics. However, this alone is insufficient. To possess practical relevance, a concept must also explain its organizational implications. Furthermore, it must be benchmarked against competing concepts to clarify distinctions. In contrast to existing literature, this comprehensive approach is undertaken in the present study, with results presented in the subsequent chapters.

23

24

CHAPTER 1: CORE COMPETENCIES & CO.

This chapter outlines the foundational premises of the core competence concept. This framework belongs to the resource-based view paradigm and, more specifically, within the dynamic capabilities paradigm that expands upon it (Teece et al. 1990). Furthermore, strategic concepts—analogous to technologies —are subject to evolutionary processes and may thus be placed chronologically (Henzler 1988). Viewed through this lens, the core competence concept resides within the *Strategic Leadership* phase—Henzler 1988:1299). Given that many established strategic constructs, such as the *experience curve* and *product portfolio*, are grounded in orthodox economic theory, these will be briefly reviewed. This comparison is essential to explain the distinctions between orthodox economic thought and the core competence perspective. Subsequently, selected concepts will be examined in greater detail to determine, in the concluding section, their implications for the conceptualization of the firm.

§ 1.1 THE CORE COMPETENCE CONCEPT AND ITS POSITIONING

The core competence concept is based on the unique capabilities of the firm. These capabilities form the firm's competitive advantage and require rigorous protection. Consequently, this theoretical lineage argues inter-firm differences as its point of departure, eschewing the "black box" treatment characteristic of orthodox economic perspectives (Nelson 1991:64). This approach has become more important in response to the heightened environmental turbulence and internal complexity currently confronting organizations (Henzler 1988:1298). In such an environment, firms seek stability, a state that can be achieved through a focus on core competencies. This need goes beyond traditional strategic planning, requiring strategic leadership (Henzler 1988:1299). To explain this shift, the foundational basic assumptions of core competence concepts are presented and then situated within theoretical paradigms, correlated with the temporal evolution of strategic thought.

§ 1.1.1 THE CORE COMPETENCE CONCEPT

Inter-firm differences arise from the historical accumulation of heterogeneous resources. These resources include not only physical assets but also—more significantly—intangible organizational capabilities developed through internal learning processes. For competitors to replicate these assets, they must undergo the same learning processes experienced by the originating firm (Collis 1991:50). This temporal advantage allows firms the opportunity to achieve competitive superiority by focusing on expanding these firm-specific assets (Dierickx & Cool 1989:1507).

Within the literature adopting this perspective, these firm-specific assets are conceptualized in a variety of ways. Itami (1987) identifies *invisible assets*, such as reputation, technological knowledge, and brand equity. Prahalad and Hamel (1990) define *core competencies* as bundles of knowledge emerging from *"the collective learning in an organization"* (Prahalad & Hamel 1990:82). Stalk et al. characterize internal strategic processes as the firm's *core capabilities*, arguing that such processes become strategic when they deliver customer value. Alternative terminologies include *distinctive competences* (Andrews 1971; Ansoff 1987), *strategic capability* (Lenz 1980), *drivers* (Porter 1991), and *strategic assets* (Amit & Schoemaker 1993).

A unifying theme among these concepts is the need for strategic management to focus on unique, firm-specific knowledge and capabilities. This focus is necessitated by an increasingly turbulent and complex corporate environment driven by rapid technological shifts, abbreviated product life cycles, accelerated knowledge diffusion, and volatile customer preferences. *"In such an environment, the essence of strategy is not the structure of a company's products and markets but the dynamics of its behaviour. And the goal is to identify and develop the hard-to-imitate organizational capabilities that distinguish a company from its competitors in the eyes of the customer"* (Stalk et al. 1992:62). Consequently, defining strategy in terms of products and markets becomes increasingly tenuous, as these variables are in constant flux. In this context, focusing on core competencies gives a more stable strategic perspective; these competencies function as the genesis for a diverse array of products across various markets, are manifest in the value ascribed by customers, and remain difficult to imitate (Prahalad & Hamel 1990:83–84).

The core competence concept thus adopts a distinct *inside-out* strategic orientation: strategy is based on firm-specific competencies, which are then leveraged to identify profitable market opportunities (Grant 1991:115). This contrasts with the prevalent *outside-in* approach influenced by Porter (1980), which focus on identifying structurally attractive markets before aligning production capabilities to serve them. Core competence management mandates the maximal use of competencies. Unlike physical assets, core competencies do not depreciate with use; rather, they are enhanced through frequent application, as this generates new knowledge and experience (Prahalad & Hamel 1990:82). Critically, core competencies are inherently cross-functional and transcend Strategic Business Units (SBUs). They cannot be compartmentalized within a single department or product line; they form the collective intellectual property of the firm.

§ 1.1.2 POSITIONING IN TIME

The historical trajectory of strategic concepts may be placed within an environmental framework (Henzler 1988:1286; based on internal McKinsey documentation, see also Gluck et al. 1982). Strategic concepts evolve in direct response to environmental pressures.

Figure 1.1

	Financial Planning (Finanzplanung)	Long-term-Planning (Langfristplanung)	Strategic Planning (Strategische Planung)	Strategic Leadership (Strategische Führung)
Environment (Umfeld)	Stability (Stabilität)	Change (Veränderung)	Instability (Instabilität)	Surprise (Überaschung)
Company Complexity (Komplexität des Unternehmens)	Low (Niedrich)	Medium (Mittel)	High (Hoch)	Very High (Ser hoch)

Source: Henzler 1988:1298

The genesis of modern strategic concepts is traceable to the early 1960s, arising as a response to significant shifts in the business environment. Key drivers included volatile business cycles, the dissolution of the Bretton Woods system, and a need to pivot from producer-centric to consumer-centric markets. Concurrently, the firm itself underwent structural transformation. Motivated by risk diversification and the prevailing managerial doctrine that management skills were transferrable regardless of market or product specificity, highly diversified conglomerates emerged. Consequently, established decision-making methodologies proved inadequate to address these internal and external fluctuations.

Existing decision-making frameworks—encompassing product life cycle analysis and budgeting (*Financial Planning*) were augmented with concepts acknowledging that distinct product/market combinations possess divergent growth rates. This shift recognized that historical trends are not reliable predictors of the future and that external variables require rigorous scrutiny. The strategic concepts emerging from this period included the *experience curve*, *portfolio planning*, and *diversification strategies*, all of which are categorized under *Long-term Planning* (Henzler 1988:1288–1292).

By the late 1970s, the strategic landscape was reshaped by the emergence of novel concepts that broadened the scope of strategic thought. This evolution was again driven by environmental factors: firms possessed sufficient equity and debt capital, markets were approaching saturation, and globalization was accelerating. Consequently, intensifying competitive pressure necessitated frameworks capable of mitigating these forces. This need drove a shift toward thinking in terms of competitive advantage, incorporating industry dynamics into strategic decision-making. These concepts are collectively characterized as *Strategic Planning*.

Porter's framework is arguably the most prominent example of this era. As he argues: *"The goal of competitive strategy for a business unit is to find a position in the industry where the company can best defend itself against ... competitive [industry] forces or can influence them in its favor"* (Porter 1980:4). In addition to established tools such as *product life cycle* and *portfolio analysis*, strategy formulation began to integrate creative market and industry analyses, as well as assessments of customer and competitive positioning (Henzler 1988:1292–1294).

By the late 1980s, these concepts appeared to reach a point of saturation, rendered insufficient by an increasingly dynamic corporate environment. The globalization of trade and enterprise intensified, trade barriers diminished (via GATT, EC, etc.), and abrupt technological shifts disrupted existing markets. Simultaneously, consumer markets fragmented, customer demands escalated, and product life cycles shortened further. In this context, the strategic value of market positioning declined due to the difficulty of defense and the transience of market definitions. Henzler argues that in such a dynamic environment, *Strategic Leadership* assumes critical importance. This approach is essential for embedding strategic capabilities broadly across the firm and utilizing fluid organizational forms adapted to constant change (Henzler 1988:1299). The core competence concept resides within this category, as it addresses heightened environmental dynamics by shifting focus away from static market positions and functional structures. Instead, it focus on knowledge and capability positions that transcend functional boundaries.

Crucially, Henzler notes that emerging concepts do not supplant their predecessors; rather, they function as supplements and correctives (Henzler 1988:1299). Therefore, the core competence concept is not a substitute for existing forms of strategic management, but rather a complementary addition to the strategic canon.

§ 1.1.3 POSITIONING ACCORDING TO PARADIGMS

Teece et al. (1990) situate the core competence concept within a model-based framework. They distinguish three existing paradigms—shielding the firm from competitive forces, strategic behavior, and the resource-based view—while proposing a fourth: the dynamic capabilities approach (1990:1). Correlating this model-based classification with the chronological evolution discussed previously suggests the following taxonomy: The *Strategic Planning* phase corresponds clearly with the competitive forces paradigm. While both the strategic behavior and the resource-based view paradigms attempt to capture greater dynamism than the competitive forces model, they remain insufficient in fully encompassing environmental flux. Consequently, they may be viewed as transitional concepts leading toward the *Strategic Leadership* phase, which houses the dynamic capabilities paradigm. It is argued that this latter approach possesses the requisite potential to address the environmental dynamics confronting contemporary firms.

Teece et al. (1990:3) observe that the competitive forces paradigm, pioneered by Porter (1980), remains dominant. The central premise of this paradigm is that the firm's environment—specifically the industry—dictates its strategy. Accordingly, the objective of strategy formulation is to align the firm with its environment, as the industry establishes the *rules of the game* for competition. These rules are governed by five forces: industry competitors, buyers, suppliers, substitutes, and potential entrants. At the national level, the *diamond* model functions as the foundational determinant of firm development (Porter 1990). Its critical factors include the intensity of competition, factor conditions, demand conditions, and related/supporting industries. The ultimate objective of Porter's analysis is the creation of a quasi-monopoly position, achieved either through insulation from competitive forces or by exerting control over them. Within Porter's framework, inter-firm differences between firms is primarily a function of scale and the concomitant ability to lower production costs. To the extent that firm-specific assets are acknowledged, they are located at the functional or staff level (value chain: Porter 1985).

The second paradigm centers on strategic behavior, attempting to model dynamics through the lens of strategic moves. The primary analytical instrument employed is game theory, which seeks to explain the actions of individuals and firms in scenarios of cooperation and conflict. It investigates potential behaviors, normative actions, and resultant outcomes. Within game theory, a firm's optimal choice depends on the choices of others, as these interdependent decisions dictate the consequences of any single action. In this context, firms are viewed as possessing high optionality, characterized by their cost positions, reputations, and other asset holdings. Operating under the assumption of profit maximization, they typically exhibit non-cooperative behavior. The focus is on committed competition; behavior is deemed strategic only if it is irreversible or reversible only at significant cost. The authors identify a critical limitation in this theory: the neglect of unique capability development—a factor that receives only marginal attention even in Porter's framework. Game theory generally predicates its models on the assumption of homogeneous firm capabilities. Furthermore, the theoretical emphasis tends toward static product-market positions rather than developing the unique capabilities that underpin superior positioning. Teece et al. argue that this focus inevitably leads to short-term strategies based merely on the exploitation of existing assets.

The third paradigm, the resource-based view, shifts the focus to the firm's unique capabilities and resources. This perspective argues that firms possessing superior capabilities or organizational structures achieve profitability through lower cost structures or the delivery of demonstrably superior product quality. A firm's strength comes from the cumulative experience acquired in the production and marketing of a specific product line—strength rooted in personnel, management, and coordination. Consequently, a firm's potential is constrained not only by environmental opportunities but also by its internal capacities in finance, production, and marketing. The argument extends to posit that a firm's success and future evolution depend on identifying capabilities that facilitate genuine differentiation. The contrast with the competitive forces paradigm is distinct. The latter focus on identifying structurally attractive industries, followed by the selection of an entry strategy based on competitors' rational moves, and finally, acquiring requisite resources. In that framework, resource acquisition is treated as trivial, under the assumption that all necessary resources are readily available via market mechanisms.

Conversely, the resource-based view treats firms as heterogeneous entities regarding their resources and capabilities. This differences between firms is critical for three reasons: First, the construction of unique capabilities and (invisible) resources is a complex, path-dependent process. Second, certain assets—such as tacit know-how—are non-tradable (Polanyi 1983). Third, even if such assets were tradable, their ubiquity would negate any potential for competitive advantage. Consequently, this approach proceeds from an opposite assumption. In contrast to the "outside-in" methodology of the competitive forces paradigm, the resource-based view paradigm adopts an "inside-out" orientation (see Figure 1.2).

The primary need is to identify the firm's unique resources, followed by the determination of markets where these resources will yield maximal returns. This perspective reframes the logic of vertical integration and diversification; both strategies are recognized as potentially critical for the effective leverage of firm-specific capabilities and resources.

The resource-based view approach also addresses developing novel capabilities. Given that competitive positioning depends on the expansion and cultivation of capabilities, the acquisition, accumulation, and organizational learning processes become paramount. It is in this domain that the authors identify the most significant contribution of the resource-based view, designating it the *dynamic capabilities approach*. This does not form a distinct paradigm but rather an extension of the resource-based foundation. The authors posit that their dynamic capabilities approach is synonymous with the core competence concept of Prahalad and Hamel (see § 1.3.4). This framework, situated within the *Strategic Leadership*, is the analytical point of departure for § 1.3 and subsequent chapters.

Figure 1.2

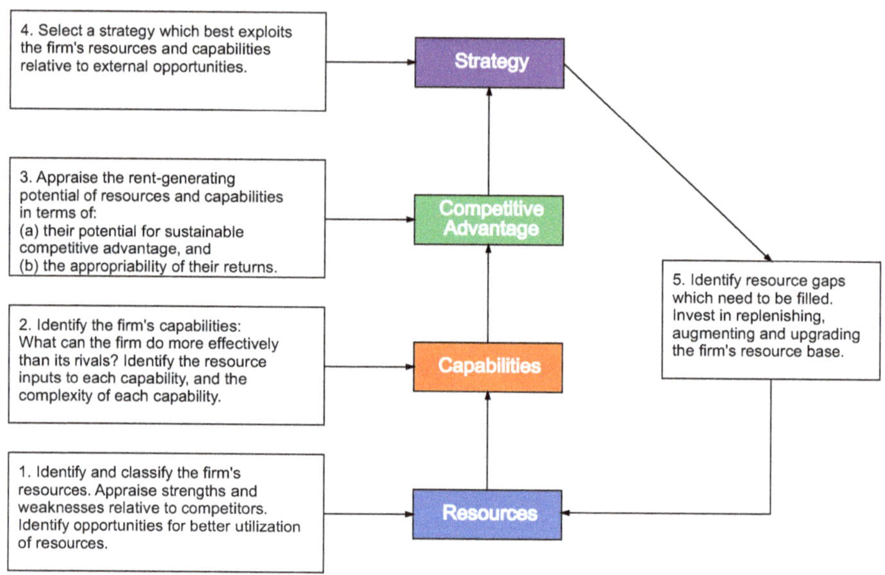

Source: Grant 1991:115

§ 1.2 ORTHODOX ECONOMIC THEORIES

The initial three phases in the evolution of strategic management concepts were heavily influenced by orthodox economic theories regarding the firm (Collis 1991:49–50). In this tradition, the firm is conceptualized as a 'black box', with analysis focused exclusively on market outcomes. Firms are assumed to possess homogenous characteristics, leaving scant room for differentiation. As Nelson (1991:61) notes: "…*economists tend to see firms as players in a multi actor economic game, and their interest is in the game and its outcomes, rather than in the particular play or performance of individual firms*". Given their influence on contemporary management thought, the primary economic perspectives are briefly outlined herein. This review establishes a baseline for comparison with the alternative economic theories discussed in Chapter Two, which form the intellectual roots of the core competence concept.

The lineage of orthodox theory extends from Smith and Ricardo through Mill, Marshall, and Walras. Marshall is generally regarded as *"…a precursor or source of today's formal neoclassical economics"* (Nelson & Winter 1982:44). Accordingly, this discussion commences with his foundational theory and the inherent challenges he confronted. Subsequent approaches by Coase and Williamson, while attempting to build upon Marshall, remain insufficient for grounding the core competence concept. The critiques of Marshall, Coase, and Williamson, as articulated by Best (1990), are summarized below.

§ 1.2.1 MARSHALL

Marshall is renowned for formulating an equilibrium theory of price based on the interaction of supply and demand. His equilibrium framework sought to integrate exchange theory with production theory by analyzing the production costs that underpin the supply curve.

In Marshall's theory of production, entrepreneurs organize firms to transform inputs into outputs. However, the input-output relationship is governed by laws of return specific to each industry. As Marshall observes: *"…the part which nature plays in production shows a tendency to diminishing return, the part which man plays shows a tendency to increasing return"*. Furthermore, he states: *"the law of increasing return may be worded thus: - an increase of labour and capital leads generally to improved organization…"* (Marshall 1938:318).

While the concept of increasing returns to scale gives a compelling explanation for the rise of large-scale industry, integrating it with equilibrium theory presents a significant theoretical challenge. One approach is to conceptualize increasing returns as a function of technological progress. However, this renders the long-run supply curve a function of time, whereas the demand curve remains a function of output. Consequently, the demand and supply curves lack a common basis of measurement, thereby preventing the derivation of an equilibrium price.

The fundamental issue lies in the inherent asymmetry between demand and supply. Movements along the demand curve do not shift the curve itself; however, movement along an upward-sloping supply curve implies a cost increase in at least one factor of production. This necessitates a rise in production costs for other goods utilizing that same factor, thereby altering their equilibrium prices. These price shifts essentially feedback to affect the demand for the original product. Consequently, isolating the demand and supply conditions of a single industry is impossible without assuming that the inputs driving the supply curve do not recur in the cost structures of other products.

Two theoretical resolutions exist. The first preserves price theory by discarding Marshall's partial equilibrium in favor of general equilibrium theory. The drawback, however, is that establishing equilibrium prices excludes the possibility of increasing returns. The second option abandons the assumption of perfect competition, arguing instead that firms set prices within specific margins around an equilibrium point. While this accommodates increasing returns, it simultaneously undermines equilibrium price theory, as the absence of perfect competition theoretically permits unbounded firm growth.

§ 1.2.2 COASE

Coase proposed a solution by delineating the determinants of firm size via Marshall's concept of marginal substitution. He argued that economic activity in a capitalist system is coordinated through two distinct mechanisms: spontaneously via the market price mechanism, or consciously through hierarchical relationships within the firm.

Coase establishes a rationale for the firm by relaxing a core assumption of general equilibrium theory: the ubiquity of markets for all current and future goods. While current supply and demand may be known, the future remains opaque and uncertain. Although uncertainty influences firm emergence, it fails to delineate the specific boundary between internal execution and market procurement. Coase resolves this via the concept of transaction costs.

Both coordination ways—market and firm—incur administrative transaction costs. Firms exist where the cost of internal transaction execution is lower than that of market mediation. Applying Marshall's principle of marginal substitution, Coase concludes that an equilibrium exists between firm and market where the marginal costs of each transaction mode are equal.

Coase's analysis, however, remains highly schematic. For instance, he attributes the limits of firm size primarily to diminishing returns to management without elucidating the underlying causal mechanisms. Furthermore, if internalizing activities remains advantageous until a monopoly is established, the competitive theory of price—and the associated process of continuous marginal substitution upon which Coase's concept relies—is rendered conceptually unstable. Best (1990) concludes that this resolution remains suboptimal.

§ 1.2.3 WILLIAMSON

Williamson critiques the conventional conceptualization of the firm as a production function, proposing instead the view of the firm as a governance structure. He modifies standard behavioral assumptions by introducing the concepts of opportunism and bounded rationality, while qualifying assumptions regarding perfect competition and complete information. Defining opportunism as *self-interest seeking with guile* (Williamson 1975:26), he places these behavioral propositions at the core of his rationale for the firm's existence.

Williamson centers his analysis on the firm's make-or-buy decision. Internalization occurs under conditions of asset specificity and/or demand externality. Asset specificity reduces perfect competition to a bilateral monopoly, complicating equilibrium price determination. Demand externalities provide a second impetus for internalization; where market coordination fails to sufficiently guarantee product quality, the firm may opt to organize the activity internally.

Consequently, the existence of the firm results from market failure. Firms emerge to mitigate or exploit market imperfections arising from bounded rationality and opportunism. Similarly, Williamson attributes the existence of conglomerates to imperfections within capital markets.

While conceptualizing the firm as a governance structure rather than a production function gives distinct advantages, this governance perspective remains divorced from actual production activities. Best therefore concludes that "*(a) theory of the firm… must move beyond considerations of coordination with concepts that allow for links between governance structure and production performance*" (Best 1990:115).

Although these orthodox economic theories underpinned the first three phases of Henzler's framework, they fail to provide adequate theoretical departure points for the core competence concept. Chapter Two will effectively address this gap by discussing the theories of Schumpeter (1987), Penrose (1972), and Nelson & Winter (1982), which offer an alternative economic perspective and substantive support for core competence theory.

§ 1.3 CONCEPTS FOR THE STRATEGIC LEADERSHIP PHASE

This section examines concepts that either facilitate a transition from the *Strategic Planning* phase to the *Strategic Leadership* phase or are already firmly situated within the latter. Porter's (1991) concept of *drivers* is a transitional mechanism between the plannings phase and the leadership phase. Similarly, Itami's (1987) concept of *invisible assets*, while primarily aligned with the resource-based paradigm, incorporates distinct elements attributable to the dynamic capabilities paradigm. Conversely, the *core competence concept* of Prahalad and Hamel (1990), the *resource-based analysis* of Collis (1991), and the *core capability concept* of Stalk et al. (1992) are representative of the *Strategic Leadership* and the *dynamic capabilities* approach.

§ 1.3.1 DRIVERS

In his article *"Towards a dynamic theory of strategy"* (Porter 1991), Porter synthesizes his prior work to examine the origins of firm success. At the macro level, he argues that firm success is a function of two primary variables: the attractiveness of the industry in which the firm competes and its relative position therein. Industry attractiveness is assessed via the five-forces model (Porter 1980), while relative position is defined by competitive advantage (cost leadership, differentiation) and competitive scope (broad vs. focused).

Porter poses a critical inquiry: "where does the relative position of a firm come from?" To address this, he dissects the concepts of cost, differentiation, and scope, mapping them to the firm's activities. A firm is conceptualized as a collection of discrete yet interrelated economic activities. Competitive advantage comes from the firm's ability to perform these collective activities at a lower cost or to execute specific activities in a unique manner that distinguishes it from competitors. Porter models these activities within a value chain and a value system (comprising the value chains of all industry actors). However, this invites a deeper causal question: "*Why is a firm capable of performing activities at a lower cost or in a unique manner?*" Porter's response is the concept of *drivers*, which he defines as "*…structural determinants of differences among competitors in the cost or buyer of activities or group of activities (…) Only by moving to the level of underlying drivers can the true sources of competitive advantage be identified*" (Porter 1991:104). He identifies the primary drivers as scale, cumulative learning, linkages between activities, capacity use patterns over the cycle, location, investment timing, vertical integration, institutional factors, and discretionary firm policy regarding activity configuration. The specific mix and weight of these drivers vary by activity, firm, and industry (1991:104).

However, this explanation remains incomplete. Porter characterizes the analysis thus far as the *cross-sectional problem*. Yet, the causal inquiry persists: "Why do certain firms achieve favorable positioning regarding specific drivers, and how do they attain and sustain these positions while others fail?" The cross-sectional problem effectively analyzes the status quo and strategies for leveraging it, but it fails to explain the trajectory by which that state was reached. This temporal dimension is what Porter terms the *longitudinal problem*.

Porter identifies two factors that address this longitudinal problem. The first is initial conditions, encompassing environmental factors (cf. the *diamond*, Porter 1990) and internal attributes such as firm history, reputation, and accumulated capabilities. These conditions constrain and shape the feasible set of strategic choices. The second factor includes managerial choices made independently of initial conditions. Pure managerial discretion drives the creation of capabilities and resources requisite for new strategy implementation. Notably, historical management choices underpin all internal initial conditions. However, tracing the causal chain further reveals that management choices and internal conditions are ultimately influenced by external initial conditions—specifically, the *diamond* context within which the firm originates.

Porter gives a somewhat overly simple conclusion, asserting that success is ultimately based on the generation of novel ideas. He observes: "*The most successful firms are notable in employing imagination to define a new position, or find new value in whatever starting position they have*" (Porter 1991:106). While logically sound, this assertion fails to explain the mechanism by which new positions or value are actually discovered. Regarding the theoretical positioning of this concept, this study argues that it functions as an extension of the competitive forces paradigm. This is manifest in the structure of Porter's argument, which takes competitive forces as its point of departure before iteratively applying causal inquiry.

In my assessment, Porter was compelled to acknowledge the salience of the resource-based paradigm, particularly following the significant impact of Prahalad and Hamel's work on core competencies. His subsequent objective appears to be the destabilization of this theory's foundation. Porter subsumes the core competence concept entirely under the resource-based framework, contending that these theories rely on unique resources that the firm must merely cultivate and protect. While partially accurate, this characterization fails to encompass the full scope of these theories. Resources extend beyond physical goods to include invisible or intangible assets, such as reputation, accumulated knowledge in products and processes, and learning capacity. By characterizing resources as commodities readily procurable in the market— at prices that already price-in competitive advantage—Porter fails to appreciate the Penrosian distinction of resources as productive services. Furthermore, Porter contends that resource-based theories focus exclusively on internal firm dynamics, disregarding the external environment. As he notes: *"In this respect, the paper by Prahalad and Hamel (1990) is perhaps the most inward looking and the most troubling"* (Porter 1991:108 footnote 22).

Having reduced the concept of core competence to a purchasable commodity, Porter contends that resources alone are insufficient for competitive advantage. *"It is the collective advantage gained from all resources that determines relative performance. (…) Performing an activity or group of linked activities over time creates internal skills and routines which accumulate"* (Porter 1991:108). I argue that this is precisely the insight the core competence concept offers— an insight Porter seemingly finds absent in the existing literature. *"The concept of activity drivers allows more precision in defining how resources were created. Some skills and routines emerge because of learning over time. (…) Other resources were obtained through well-timed factor purchases (timing). Still others are the result of the ability to share across units"* (Porter 1991:109). Porter appears to seek a terminological redefinition, recasting core competence as drivers, with the primary distinction being the association of the latter term with his own scholarship.

When evaluated within Henzler's positioning framework, the extent to which Porter's drivers address increased external dynamics is questionable. A close examination of the primary drivers identified by Porter reveals them to be largely positional rather than dynamic. Factors such as scale, capacity use, location, degree of vertical integration, and institutional constraints define a firm's static position. Only cumulative learning, inter-unit sharing, and activity linkages qualify as dynamic, as they facilitate acquiring new knowledge, capabilities, and experience—inputs that then fuel further learning and capability expansion.

This study argues that Porter's enumeration of drivers is inconsistent with his own definition of them as *"structural determinants of differences among competitors…"* (1991:104). The inclusion of non-structural (i.e., dynamic) determinants likely represents a strategic concession to the core competence concept. Thus, the drivers concept remains predominantly anchored in the *Strategic Planning* phase and does not qualify for classification within the *Strategic Leadership* phase.

§ 1.3.2 INVISIBLE ASSETS

The essence of successful strategy lies in what Itami terms *dynamic strategic fit*—the continuous alignment of internal and external factors with the content of the strategy itself. Strategy must be deliberately engineered to sustain this fit amidst fluctuating conditions. Itami argues that strategic fit is achieved through the effective use and efficient accumulation of the firm's *invisible assets. "Only a firm that carefully cultivates such 'assets' will be in a position to achieve and maintain a record of successful strategy"* (Itami 1987:1).

Itami defines invisible assets not as tangible, measurable resources like plant and machinery, but as intangible elements such as proprietary technology, accumulated customer intelligence, brand equity, reputation, and corporate culture. These assets are indispensable; indeed, Itami asserts that they *"… are often a firm's only real source of competitive edge that can be sustained over time"* (Itami 1987:1).

Itami illustrates this through the analogy of creating a painting. While a painter requires physical presence, funding, brushes, canvas, and paint, these factor inputs alone do not guarantee a masterpiece. The requisite differentiator is the painter's artistic capability and technique—his invisible assets. Crucially, individuals cannot be decoupled from the invisible assets (knowledge, experience, capabilities) they possess. Human resources are not merely interchangeable factor inputs; rather, they function as the *accumulators and producers of invisible assets* (Itami 1987:14).

From this perspective, the stock of invisible assets dictates the feasible set of strategic options. Prior decisions regarding asset accumulation constrain the strategies viable in the short term. Consequently, the significance of current strategy goes beyond the generation of immediate competitive advantage; it determines the future level of invisible assets, thereby establishing the foundation for future strategic optionality.

The critical nature of invisible assets is underscored by three factors (Itami 1987:12–13). First, they are arduous to construct; they cannot be readily procured in the marketplace. Their creation demands continuous investment of capital, knowledge, and time, thereby enabling genuine firm differentiation. Second, they possess the capacity for simultaneous use. Unlike a specific employee or physical space, which has no or limited concurrent use, knowledge of a technology, brand name, or reputation can be deployed concurrently across multiple domains. Thus, a single resource can generate multiple returns. Third, an invisible asset functions simultaneously as both an input and an output of a process. This dual character is pivotal in strategy formulation.

Money exhibits an analogous property: it is required to produce goods and is recouped upon their sale. Similarly, technological experience enables the execution of a process, while the execution itself augments that experience. A robust brand and reputation facilitate entry into a distribution channel; if successful, this presence further enhances reputation and brand recognition. "*When an asset…is both an input and an output in business operations, it is important not just to consider its effective use as an input in current strategy, but also to recognize that more of that asset will be accumulated as an output of business operations. (…) Effective asset use as an input is sometimes incompatible with efficient accumulation as an output. (…) Too much emphasis on effective utilization prevents efficient accumulation*" (Itami 1987:16–17). This tension is explained through the monetary analogy: an excessive focus on the effective use of funds, at the expense of their efficient accumulation, may preclude the exploitation of future opportunities due to capital constraints.

The accumulation of invisible assets occurs through two distinct mechanisms: direct and indirect. Direct accumulation is typified by for example television advertising designed to bolster brand recognition, or R&D investment directed toward technological advancement. Conversely, indirect accumulation emerges as a byproduct of routine operational activities. For example, product quality and reliability facilitate reputation building. Likewise, sales representatives interact with clients not merely to transact, but to garner intelligence regarding customer preferences and competitor performance. Such data is critical, empowering the firm to address customer needs responsively.

When a firm fails to generate additional invisible assets, it incurs a dual loss. First, its asset pool ceases to expand, whereas that of competitors may continue to grow. Second, the fundamental structure of existing invisible assets may be compromised; this trajectory typically exerts a compounding negative impact on the firm. While indirect accumulation is generally more protracted, it is simultaneously more reliable and enduring. This distinction is explained by comparing television commercials, intended to construct a brand image, with organic word-of-mouth communication. Although the latter process is far slower, it engenders greater persistence within the customer base.

Resource accumulation forms a pivotal component of strategy. *"A current strategy has to create enough resources for future strategy to be carried out. And the future strategy must make effective use of the resources amassed. With these two steps, a firm has the dynamic combinatorial effect, which is the basis of dynamic resource fit"* (Itami 1987:125). This principle underpins the core of firm growth: the creation of shared-use potential for resource deployment through dynamic synergy. First, this enables the effective accumulation and deployment of resources over an extended horizon, in a manner responsive to environmental shifts. Second, such synergy helps the effortless creation of complementary effects between products and markets. *"To generate dynamic strategy, a firm should choose activities that create invisible assets, design strategy with dynamic synergy in mind, and go beyond its current abilities to develop these invisible assets"* (Itami 1987:130).

Centering on the firm's invisible assets, the organization must achieve a dynamic strategic fit. This entails identifying five specific dimensions: customer fit, competitive fit, technological fit, resource fit, and organizational fit. These alignments must ostensibly be reflected in the firm's strategy. This is not an annual exercise but a continuous endeavor to maintain equilibrium with the perpetually shifting environment, resource base, and organizational structure.

The concept of invisible assets is rooted in the resource-based paradigm. A firm's unique resources offer the potential for differentiation from competitors and represent the source of competitive advantage. The resources central to this discussion are invisible or intangible assets—such as reputation, customer loyalty, and brand recognition—which are critical for current and future strategic options. Itami also discusses acquiring new resources and developing new capabilities and invisible assets. In this regard, he approximates the dynamic capabilities paradigm, effectively taking a preliminary step toward it. However, the dynamic capabilities paradigm places greater emphasis on the construction and expansion of core competencies. It focuses more intensely on continuous acquisition, expansion, and the associated learning processes surrounding a specific capability or knowledge domain that yields potential competitive advantage. Although Itami does not advance the analysis to this extent, his work offers an initial step in that direction.

§ 1.3.3 RESOURCE-BASED ANALYSIS

In his article *"A resource-based analysis of global competition: the case of the bearings industry"*, Collis investigates the contribution of the resource-based view of the firm to global competition and strategic management generally (1991:49). He synthesizes the premises of global competition into four points (1991:49). First, a global strategy is requisite when significant interdependencies exist between competitive positions in different countries. Second, the causes of these interdependencies, which result in competitive advantage, are identifiable. Third, a global strategy pertains to the configuration and coordination of activities. Fourth, organizational structure should be derivative of strategy. In his view, these propositions reflect the *"…mainstream economic tradition of strategic theory with its emphasis on market outcomes between ex-ante symmetrical firms, and are derived primarily from external analysis of competition in the product market. Internal organization issues are viewed as subordinate to strategic choice and a matter of static administrative efficiency"* (Collis 1991:49–50).

Drawing on a brief literature review, Collis concludes that two fundamental hypotheses regarding global competition diverge from the standard economic explanation. The first hypothesis argues that a firm's historical evolution *"…constrains its strategic choice and so will affect market outcomes"* while the second suggests that *"…complex social phenomena…can be a source of sustainable competitive advantage and will affect organization structure independently of strategic choice"* (Collis 1991:51). To operationalize these hypotheses, he identifies three elements of the resource-based view: core competence, organizational capability, and administrative heritage. He defines a core competence as *"…the vector of the irreversible assets along which the firm is uniquely advantaged"* (Collis 1991:51). He perceives this vector as multidimensional, *"…reflecting the entire system of tangible and intangible resources that the organization has in place…"* (Collis 1991:51), and notes that it is often reduced to a single dimension in descriptions. A prerequisite is that a core competence be *distinctive*, as only a unique and superior competence can form the basis of advantage. Consequently, competencies must be benchmarked against those of competitors.

Although external opportunities are uniform for every firm, internal investments in additional resources will vary because accumulated resource vectors differ. This variance explains why firms select distinct product/market combinations, and *"this implies that firms will choose product market positions that represent the best application of their core competence even if it leads to seemingly second best choices"* (Collis 1991:51).

Organizational capability *"…represents the managerial capability to continually improve and upgrade firm efficiency and effectiveness…"* and successful firms possess a collective capacity to both innovate and adapt to environmental shifts, enabling continuous improvement (Collis 1991:52). Administrative heritage indicates organizational constraints on strategic choice. *"It consists of both the intangible cultural heritage and the physical heritage of the firm"* (Collis 1991:52).

Based on these three elements, Collis formulates several hypotheses concerning inter-firm differences. These hypotheses suggest that firms may become active in structurally less attractive markets; that the country of origin influences strategic choices; that organizational structure does not follow directly from strategy; and that, due to administrative heritage, firms may make decisions that do not align with production cost optimization. Collis' case study will be reviewed in § 6.2.1.

As the title of Collis (1991) suggests, his conceptual framework is intrinsically rooted in the resource-based paradigm. While he references core competencies and cites the *collective learning* aspect of Prahalad & Hamel (1990), his discussion does not incorporate the continuous evolution of competencies within the core competence framework. He does, however, address this dimension under the rubric of organizational capability. He argues that, to achieve a collective capacity for innovation and adaptability to external shifts, "…*the firm must create dynamic routines that facilitate innovation, foster collective learning, and transfer information and skills within the organization*" (Collis 1991:52). In this regard, the concept goes beyond the resource-based paradigm and advances toward the dynamic capabilities paradigm.

§ 1.3.4 CORE COMPETENCIES

In their seminal article "*The Core Competence of the Corporation*", Prahalad & Hamel (1990) assert that conventional organizational theory views the firm as an aggregation of Strategic Business Units (SBUs); the firm is thus conceptualized as a portfolio of SBUs. An SBU is defined as an autonomous unit organized around a specific product/market combination (Dongen 1993:5). Prahalad & Hamel articulate the limitations of SBU-centric logic, noting that competitive capability is typically gauged by the price/performance ratios of current products marketed through those SBUs. However, this metric assesses competitive capability only at the present juncture, or within the immediate short term. Over the long term, competitive capability is determined by alternative metrics, specifically the capacity to rapidly develop superior or more cost-effective new products, generate novel products, or penetrate new markets. "*The real sources of advantage are to be found in management's ability to consolidate corporatewide technologies and production skills into competencies that empower individual businesses to adapt quickly to changing opportunities*" (Prahalad & Hamel 1990:81). This adaptability is needed given the relentless acceleration of environmental dynamics.

Prahalad & Hamel employ an arboreal metaphor to describe the firm (1990:82). The roots, analogous to the firm's core competencies, nourish the trunk, branches, and leaves. These core competencies sustain the trunk and main branches, which represent the firm's core products. From these main branches extend smaller branches symbolizing the SBUs. The leaves, flowers, and fruit correspond to the firm's end products. Just as the roots of a tree require sustenance, a firm's core competencies must be continuously nurtured; knowledge atrophies when unused. Unlike physical assets, where increased use precipitates wear and depreciation, core competencies exhibit an inverse relationship (1990:82). Frequent use of core competencies engenders experience, resulting in deeper, more extensive, and superior competencies. *"Core competences are the collective learning in the organization, especially how to coordinate diverse production skills and integrate multiple streams of technologies"* (Prahalad & Hamel 1990:82).

The perspective of the firm as a portfolio of SBUs necessitates complementation by a portfolio of core competencies (1990:86). Assessing a competitor's strength is impossible if one examines only end products. Prahalad & Hamel illustrate this with the example of Honda, which appears to exhibit unrelated diversification (in terms of SIC codes) across cars, motorcycles, lawn mowers, and generators. However, when one recognizes that Honda's core competencies reside in engines and power trains, the portfolio reveals a high degree of cohesiveness (1990:83).

A core competence must satisfy a minimum of three criteria (1990:84–85). First, it must provide potential access to a diverse array of markets. Second, it must deliver significant value-add to end products from the customer's perspective. Third, it must be difficult for competitors to imitate. Most Western firms rarely conceptualize competitive capability in these terms, preferring to assess it via price/performance ratios of end products. Consequently, they risk eroding or diluting their core competencies (1990:84). The intellectual capital and capabilities requisite for future product generations cannot be procured via outsourcing or OEM supply agreements. Many firms have erred by reducing investment in activities perceived merely as cost centers, believing savings could be achieved through outsourcing. However, this logic was erroneously applied to crucial components—the firm's core products. While outsourcing may offer a shortcut to temporarily securing a competitive product, it fails to contribute to expanding the people-embodied skills essential for long-term competitiveness (1990:84). The opportunity costs of losing a core competence are inherently incalculable (risking the loss of essential assets alongside the dispensable), and it is notably difficult for a firm to enter a developing market without prior investment in the requisite core competencies (1990:85). Core competencies are constructed through a process of continuous improvement and progression that may span years. Even a brief neglect of core competence development renders catching up with competitors very difficult.

The nexus between identified core competencies and end products is formed by core products; *"…the physical embodiments of one or more core competencies"* (Prahalad & Hamel 1990:85). These are the components that contribute to customer value within end products. Distinguishing this threefold structure is critical because the nature of competition varies at each level (1990:85). To establish or defend long-term leadership, a firm must likely prevail across all three levels.

At the level of core competencies, the strategic objective is the attainment of global leadership in the design and development of specific product functionalities. To sustain this leadership, firms strive to maximize their share of global core product production. Through this mechanism, the firm acquires the financial resources, capabilities, and experience necessary to expand and refine its core competencies. Such a dominant position is also pivotal for developing new markets and innovating new applications for core competencies. In turn, core competencies and the market position of core products exert a significant influence on the price/performance ratios of end products.

Prahalad & Hamel contend that to ensure success, firms must relinquish strict SBU-centric thinking, arguing that the associated costs are prohibitive. Establishing core competencies and a robust position in the global market for core products demands substantial, long-term investments for which no single SBU assumes responsibility. Consequently, the firm risks underinvesting in core competencies and core products. Furthermore, SBU managers are disinclined to share unique competencies and talent with other SBUs, perceiving these resources as proprietary to their unit or fearing they will not be returned. This phenomenon results in what Prahalad & Hamel term *imprisoned resources*. If core competencies remain unrecognized, SBUs will focus exclusively on innovations aligned with their immediate interests, resulting in marginal product line extensions or geographic expansion while neglecting hybrid opportunities that leverage competencies from other SBUs.

This myopia undermines the firm's competitiveness, a trajectory that top management is tasked with reversing. *"Top management must add value by enunciating the strategic architecture that guides the competence acquisition process"* (Prahalad & Hamel 1990:91).

By emphasizing the necessity of continuously improving core competencies through collective learning, this concept aligns with the dynamic capabilities paradigm as defined by Teece et al. (1990). Indeed, Teece et al. explicitly equate the dynamic capabilities paradigm with Prahalad & Hamel's core competence concept (Teece et al. 1990:29 footnote 11).

§ 1.3.5 CORE CAPABILITIES

In early 1992, Stalk et al. introduced the concept of core capabilities and the concomitant framework of capabilities-based competition (Stalk et al. 1992). Citing numerous exemplars, they demonstrate that in many industries, the positions of incumbents have been usurped by dynamic challengers. These instances are not isolated anecdotes but are emblematic of a fundamental shift in competitive logic. The authors posit that historical competition was based on selecting and occupying distinct product or market segments to maximize market share—a viable strategy within a relatively static competitive landscape. However, driven by market fragmentation, abbreviated product life cycles, the erosion of boundaries via globalization, and a consequent proliferation of competitors, the maintenance of static positions has become increasingly arduous. In a hyper-dynamic environment, strategy must exhibit matching dynamism (1992:62).

Contemporary success hinges on anticipating market trends and rapidly addressing shifting customer needs—essentially, the capacity for velocity and flexibility. *"In such an environment, the essence of strategy is not the structure of a company's products and markets but the dynamics of its behaviour"* (Stalk et al. 1992:62). The strategic objective is the identification and cultivation of inimitable organizational capabilities that differentiate the firm from competitors in the customer's perception (1992:62).

They delineate four principles of capabilities-based competition (1992:62): 1. The locus of firm strategy shifts from products and markets to business processes. 2. Success is defined by the transformation of key business processes into strategic capabilities that consistently deliver superior customer value. 3. Firms generate these capabilities through strategic investments in support infrastructure that integrates traditional SBU functions and goes beyond SBU boundaries. 4. Given the inherently cross-functional nature of these capabilities, strategic leadership is the domain of top management.

The crux of creating strategic capabilities lies in actual customer desires and requirements. A capability qualifies as strategic only if it originates and culminates with the customer (1992:62). Furthermore, the authors contend that *new product development* forms an overly narrow definition. Product development represents merely one facet of satisfying customer needs; a more holistic perspective is *product realization*. Consequently, importance attaches not only to new product development but also to marketing and the service accompanying the product (1992:62).

As the complexity and length of the business process stream increase, the difficulty of transforming them into strategic capabilities escalates. However, successful transformation yields processes of greater value and enhanced inimitability (1992:62). Consequently, firms achieving this combine scale with flexibility to outperform competitors across five dimensions (Stalk et al. 1992:63):

- Speed: The capability to respond rapidly to customer or market demand and to integrate novel ideas and technologies into products expeditiously.

- Consistency: The capability to manufacture products that precisely satisfy customer expectations.

- Acuity: The capability to accurately assess the environmental context, thereby anticipating and addressing evolving customer needs.

- Agility: The capability to adapt simultaneously to divergent business environments.

- Innovativeness: The capability to generate novel concepts and synthesize existing elements to create new value sources.

Competition grounded in strategic capabilities affords firms opportunities to leverage both differentiation and focus (1992:65). A firm centered on its strategic capabilities can diversify across a broad spectrum of regions, products, and industries with greater coherence than the typical conglomerate. A capabilities-based firm expands through the transfer of essential processes (1992:65)—initially to new geographic territories and subsequently to new industries.

The authors distinguish the core capability concept from Prahalad & Hamel's core competence concept. They argue that core competencies represent combinations of discrete technologies and production capabilities underpinning a firm's product lines. While both concepts underscore the behavioral dimensions of strategy, core competence focuses on specific value chain segments, whereas core capability encompasses the entire value chain. Consequently, they posit that the concepts are complementary, offering potential for a grand unifying theory—a topic reserved for Chapter Five (1992:66).

The core capabilities concept is premised on business processes and their potential transformation into strategic capabilities. Creating a strategic capability mandates that the process originates and culminates with customer needs. Furthermore, it necessitates continuous investment in infrastructure designed to organize the firm around selected strategic capabilities. *"Organize around the chosen capability and make sure employees have the necessary skills and resources…"* (Stalk et al. 1992:64). This represents a critical step in becoming a capabilities-based competitor. Implicitly, this requires that the requisite capabilities undergo continuous improvement and expansion to address shifting customer needs. To achieve innovation within chosen capabilities, the dynamism of those capabilities must be even more pronounced.

Although this concept shifts the perspective somewhat from resources to processes, it retains internal capabilities as the foundational point for strategy determination. This situates the concept within the dynamic capabilities paradigm. Simultaneously, by attempting to address external firm dynamics, this concept—alongside resource-based analysis and the core competence concept—can be classified within the *Strategic Leadership* phase.

§ 1.4 PRELIMINARY CONCLUSIONS

§ 1.4.1 A DIFFERENT PERSPECTIVE ON THE FIRM

The core competence concept and allied theories posit that a firm ought to structure itself around its core competencies. The precise constitution of a core competence and the mechanisms for organizational alignment around it are deferred for the present, to be addressed in Chapters Three and Four, respectively. By nature, a core competence transcends SBU boundaries and diverges from the prevailing definition of an SBU: an autonomous organizational unit centered on a product, market, or combination thereof (Dongen 1993:7). A core competence is fundamentally a quality or capability with the generative potential to yield a diverse array of products across distinct markets. Consequently, core competence logic necessitates a reconceptualization of the firm through the lenses of quality, knowledge, and capability. From this perspective, it becomes evident that resources, the knowledge stock, and unique capabilities constitute the foundation of a firm's competitive advantage. Resources and knowledge are deemed relevant, and a capability is classified as unique or strategic, precisely when they are oriented toward the delivery of customer value.

Predicated on a firm's resources and capabilities, one assesses where competitive advantage may be realized and determines the requisite strategy. This contrasts with the outside-in approach, which prioritizes the identification of profit maximization opportunities before considering the acquisition of necessary resources and capabilities. Core competence theories contend that the latter approach is unfeasible in the short term, thus advocating for the inverse trajectory.

Given that a firm possesses a cumulative stock of knowledge, experience, and capabilities, strategy formulation must account for the reciprocal influence strategy exerts on this repository. Strategic action can augment or deplete this stock, yielding significant future implications. A firm's strategic options are contingent, in part, upon this existing stock of knowledge, experience, and capabilities. Consequently, strategy exhibits a path-dependent nature that must be consciously integrated into strategic formulation. This perspective diverges from orthodox economic theories, which posit firms as largely homogeneous market actors capable of acquiring any technology and entering arbitrary markets at any given juncture.

The development, maintenance, and expansion of these core competencies mandate the cultivation of a collective learning process within the firm. This collective learning transcends SBU boundaries and centers on the firm's core competencies. Individual employee learning is insufficient; rather, it is collective learning—and by extension, the firm's collective memory—that dictates the potential for knowledge expansion, improvement, and innovation. This capacity is essential to navigate heightened external dynamics regarding products (shortened Product Life Cycles: Von Braun 1990; 1991), markets (fragmentation, globalization: Porter 1990), and technologies (accelerated knowledge diffusion: Mansfield 1969; Hill and Utterback 1979).

In my assessment, these constitute the salient tenets of core competence theories that offer a distinct perspective on the firm. The subsequent section briefly outlines the implications of this perspective for various legacy concepts.

§ 1.4.2 WHAT ARE DIFFERENCES WITH LEGACY CONCEPTS?

This section outlines the differing perspectives between the core competence concept and widely used traditional frameworks. Chapter Five will explore this topic in greater depth, examining the extent to which these legacy concepts remain applicable within the core competence paradigm and identifying necessary modifications.

Traditional strategic frameworks are predicated on SBU logic, exemplified by the *growth/share product portfolio*. Within this model, products or entire SBUs are classified according to market growth and relative market share. Based on this classification, normative strategies are prescribed contingent upon the position of the product or SBU (Abell and Hammond 1988). While the product portfolio technique has garnered significant critique (e.g., Seeger 1984), its continued relevance is questionable given the aforementioned dynamics of products and markets. Both products and market definitions exhibit increasingly abbreviated lifespans. As Prahalad & Hamel (1990:86) suggest, it is preferable to conceptualize a firm's competence portfolio, although they do not further specify the operationalization of this construct. A competence portfolio may yield a more stable and lucid depiction of a firm's position than one based on products. Furthermore, this approach necessitates identifying competitors with comparable competencies rather than merely comparable products, thereby providing superior insight into potential competitive threats. When Xerox pioneered xerography, thereby creating the copier market, it failed to consider Canon, a camera manufacturer, as a rival. Within a product portfolio framework, such a comparison would be incongruous. However, a competence portfolio reveals that both product lines rely on shared knowledge domains, such as optical technologies. In this respect, Canon was indeed a latent competitor. This potentiality materialized significantly; between 1976 and 1982, Canon introduced over 90 copier models, eroding Xerox's share of the mid-range copier market by 50% (Stalk et al. 1992:61).

The *value chain* concept is similarly oriented toward SBU logic. An SBU is an independent unit organized around products and markets. For each SBU, a value chain may be constructed to distinguish between primary activities (inbound and outbound logistics, marketing, etc.) and support activities (human resource management, technology management, etc.). The efficacy of this concept is constrained as it is confined to conceptualization at the SBU level. Core competencies cut across SBU boundaries and, by definition, must be analyzed at the firm level. However, developing a single, high-level value chain for the entire firm risks obscuring critical information. A firm may possess multiple core competencies that a unitary value chain fails to illuminate. Consequently, a distinct value chain should be delineated for each core competence.

Diversification strategies and *synergy* are conceptualized differently within the core competence concept.. Ansoff distinguishes four diversification strategies based on products and markets (Ansoff 1965:109). As previously noted, the variables of product and market possess diminished relevance within core competence theory. Within this paradigm, a single core competence can underpin the production and delivery of a wide variety of products to diverse markets. Thus, synergy is achieved not merely through shared production costs across products, but through the effective leverage of core competence. Synergy is generated via the expansion and enhancement of knowledge, experience, and capabilities, which are reflected in firm processes and the resulting products. This logic extends to vertical integration. In conventional economic theory, the internalization or externalization of an activity is evaluated from a cost perspective (internal costs versus external price plus transaction costs; Jarillo 1988:35). In the core competence concept, one evaluates an activity's contribution to the stock of knowledge and experience, and its status as part of a strategic business process. These factors determine whether an activity is internalized or externalized. The long-term cost of divesting a strategic activity may far exceed the immediate differential between internal and external costs.

Finally, attention is given to the *experience curve*. At first glance, this appears to correspond with the core competence concept and the collective learning effects that occur within it. This is only partly true. The standard experience curve is a purely economically applied instrument, in the sense that it relates production volume to production costs per unit. As volume increases, production costs per unit decline, as do marketing and administrative costs. In addition, there is also an experience effect. This includes the experience gained by employees through identifying small production improvements, more efficient use of materials, and similar factors. However, this is only one component of the core competence concept. The latter goes much further than production knowledge and experience, which in the experience curve is more or less regarded as a favorable side effect. It concerns a focus of the entire firm on expanding knowledge and increasing experience and capabilities across the full range of a particular competence and/or business process. It is once again more than merely deepening knowledge within a particular functional discipline; it lies precisely in integrating, coordinating, and upgrading multiple disciplines around a particular theme.

CHAPTER 2: INTELLECTUAL ROOTS

This chapter explores the intellectual lineage of the core competence concept. The theories under consideration diverge significantly from the orthodox frameworks addressed in § 1.2. Initially, the discussion outlines the inadequacies of orthodox theories in explicating the core competence concept, then identifying more aligned alternative economic theories. It is argued that the intellectual foundations of this concept reside in the works of Schumpeter (1987), Penrose (1972), and Nelson & Winter (1982). Drawing upon these theoretical frameworks, several defining characteristics of core competence theory are articulated, specifically relating to the *learning organization*, *path dependency*, and the *selection-environment*.

§ 2.1 CRITICISM OF ORTHODOX ECONOMIC THEORIES

Nelson & Winter (1982:12–13) examine the foundational assumptions of orthodox economic theories. A cornerstone of these paradigms is maximization behavior, which includes three integral components: the existence of a general objective, a well-defined choice set, and rational choice. In orthodox theory, the objective is typically profit maximization. A well-defined choice set implies the firm's capacity to evaluate and weigh all potential alternatives. Rational choice is then exercised in favor of the alternative that optimally satisfies the objective. The second pillar of orthodox economic theory is *equilibrium*. Market demand and supply curves represent aggregations of the behavioral rules of individual buyers and sellers, outlining transaction quantities at strictly defined price levels. Consequently, market price, and the resulting behavior of market actors, is determined by demand-supply equilibrium conditions.

Various scholars (Best 1990; Nelson & Winter 1982; Dankbaar et al. 1990; Nelson 1991) conclude that orthodox theories, in their pursuit of equilibrium, fail to account for structural economic and technological fluxes. These factors are treated as external variables and are excluded from the primary models. Attempts to reconcile this within orthodox frameworks typically assume that behavioral adaptations in firms occur instantaneously and that shifts in market conditions—and the resulting equilibria—are perfectly predictable by all agents. However, a more pragmatic assumption argues that firms require a temporal buffer to respond, acting on imperfect information regarding future market conditions (Nelson & Winter 1982:24). Such a response—for instance, to technological change—scarcely qualifies as maximization, as firms possess only incomplete information and thus lack a well-defined choice set. Furthermore, the industry effectively exists in a state of temporary disequilibrium. Orthodox theories generally fail to recognize this state, acknowledging, at most, a shifting equilibrium. While equilibrium theorists have attempted to address this via ad hoc models— assuming firms facing suboptimal conditions can execute precise policy adjustments—these models fundamentally rely on the optimization of adjustment costs relative to time. This, however, repeatedly implies the possession of perfect information and the capacity for perfect prediction.

Concerning the profit objective, it is arguable that alternative objectives coexist (Nelson & Winter 1982:53). Furthermore, specific objectives may be not aligned—for example, minimizing environmental impact versus minimizing production costs. Consequently, formulating a single, maximizable global function is unfeasible. Instead, the phenomenon of *satisficing* prevails (Nelson & Winter 1982:31). While orthodox theory argues that a firm cannot function without profit maximization (as it would lack purpose), Nelson & Winter contend that *"possession of a complete, clearly defined objective function is not a necessary condition for business operation in the real world; all that is required is a procedure for determining the action to be taken"* (1982:57). Orthodox theory explains firm behavior through the lens of maximizing choices, treating information-processing capacity as essentially costless and infinite. However, the finite information-processing capacity of individuals and firms forms the problem of *bounded rationality*: human cognitive limitations render true maximization or optimization impossible, resulting in *satisficing*. *"The case against maximizing behaviour focused on the faulty assumption of the closed decision model. In essence, objectives tend to be dynamic rather than fixed or unchanging. The known set of alternatives is always incomplete because of the impossibility of obtaining perfect information. And the cognitive limitations of human beings preclude serious considerations of a large number of alternatives. Many of the variables in a decision-making situation cannot be easily quantified. And it is virtually impossible to successfully implement any type of decision that has external effects without considering environmental forces"* (Harrison 1987:135).

Orthodox theory further fails to acknowledge differences between firms in firm decision-making mechanisms and the variable constraints and costs attached thereto. This deficiency stems from the *black box* conceptualization of the firm inherent in orthodox models (Nelson 1991:64). Since the formulation of equilibrium theory, the analytical focus has remained on market resource allocation: the firm is reduced to a transformation mechanism converting inputs to outputs. Firms are assumed to operate within markets characterized by perfect competition and perfect information, possessing fixed choice sets from which optimal actions are readily selected. This framework implies an impossibility for firms to exhibit differential responses to external shifts. The firm is defined as a production set—a description of the state of knowledge regarding transformation possibilities (Nelson & Winter 1982:60). Orthodox theory argues that this knowledge is universally accessible, implying that all knowledge is codifiable and transferable. However, specific knowledge domains are tacit (Polanyi 1983), resisting transfer as they exist below the level of conscious articulation (e.g., experience and intuition). Firms accumulate varying reservoirs of this tacit knowledge, creating substantive inter-firm differences. Furthermore, the temporal dynamics of knowledge acquisition are marginalized in orthodox theories. Conversely, firms engage in diverse R&D trajectories, resulting in distinct production sets. *"For the sake of formal adherence to the orthodox canon, growth theory abstracted from the uncertainty, the transient gains and losses, the uneven, groping character of technical advance, and the diversity of firm characteristics and its strategies - that is, from the key features of the capitalist dynamic"* (Nelson & Winter 1982:28).

§ 2.2 FOUNDATIONAL PILLARS OF THE CORE COMPETENCE CONCEPT

The preceding analysis explains the fundamental antithesis between orthodox economic theories and the core competence concept. This section examines the theories of Schumpeter, Penrose, and Nelson & Winter. Proceeding from assumptions that diverge from orthodox doctrine, these theories exhibit distinct elements aligned with core competence theory. The structural relationship among these theories is stratified as follows:

Schumpeter addresses the macroeconomic tier, Penrose represents the micro-organizational tier, and Nelson & Winter, through their evolutionary economic theory, operate at the meso-level.

§ 2.2.1 THE SCHUMPETERIAN FIRM AND ENVIRONMENT

Schumpeter formulated a theoretical counterargument to Marshallian equilibrium theory. While equilibrium frameworks strive for an ideal of continuity—thereby neglecting structural flux and negating the agency of firm strategy—Schumpeter equates continuity with stagnation, arguing instead an ideal of perpetual innovation and change. The impetus of innovation in driving down costs and prices, irrespective of monopoly conditions, dominates firm behavior (Best 1990:118). Even if static orthodox theories were adapted into a disequilibrium framework featuring imperfect competition, they would remain insufficient to capture the essence of Schumpeterian competition and the capitalist process (Best 1990:118). Best (1990:118–121) outlines several comparative distinctions.

Price Competition versus Creative Destruction Price competition forms only a fraction of economic dynamics. As Schumpeter articulates: "*…in capitalist reality as distinguished from its textbook picture, it is not that kind of [price] competition which counts but the competition from the new commodity, the new technology, the new source of supply, the new type of organization…- competition which commands a decisive cost or quality advantage and which strikes not at the margins of the profits and the outputs of the existing firms but at their foundations and their very lives*" (Schumpeter 1987:84). Given that product design, technology, organizational structure, and market configuration are mutable, they must be integral to strategic firm action; consequently, they fall within the purview of Schumpeterian economic analysis. Here, capitalism is driven not by customers selecting among existing products based on marginal utility and parametric price ratios, nor by the entrepreneur's marginal make-or-buy decisions, but rather by the forces of creative destruction: a "*…process of industrial mutation…that incessantly revolutionizes the economic structure from within, incessantly destroying the old one, incessantly creating a new one. This process of Creative Destruction is the essential fact about capitalism*" (Schumpeter 1942:83).

Efficiency versus Innovation Schumpeter defines innovation as the establishment of a novel production function. While equilibrium theories concentrate on output variations resulting from input changes, Schumpeter focuses on variations in the form of the production function itself. Crucially, he does not restrict his analysis to changes within a static production function, as this would imply product immutability. Instead, competition involving new products, processes, and organizational forms, form the core of the capitalist process and relies on strategic decision-making. It is the threat of obsolescence, rather than price competition, that disciplines the capitalist.

The Administrative Coordinator versus the Entrepreneur Analysis must center on structural change rather than equilibrium processes. As Schumpeter argues: *"Current economic theory is almost wholly a theory of the administration of a given industrial apparatus. But much more important than the manner in which capitalism administers given industrial structures is the manner in which it creates them"* (Schumpeter 1942:84). The entrepreneur functions as the initiator, carrier, and implementer of new ideas; indeed, every firm is founded upon a specific idea. Consequently, the entrepreneur is of paramount importance in Schumpeter's framework.

By prioritizing the entrepreneur, Schumpeter de-emphasizes the role of the administrator. This administrator, alongside the customer, is characterized by Best as the *persona dramatis* of equilibrium theory. The entrepreneur is driven not to maximize profits via the substitution of homogeneous production factors for a static product, but rather to innovate across product designs, production processes, and organizational forms. While the profit maximization assumption operates within existing rules, the entrepreneurial assumption is based on a force that generates new rules for new games.

The Ideal of Perfect Competition Schumpeter radically departs from the ideal of perfect competition. He asserts: *"perfect competition is not only impossible but inferior, and has no title to being set up as a model of ideal efficiency"* (Schumpeter 1942:106). Perfect competition allows firms minimal latitude to exploit opportunities. Firms incapable of embedding an organizational capability to anticipate change and seize opportunities will inevitably succumb to competitors that possess such agility, regardless of the efficiency with which the former allocate resources under static conditions.

To anticipate change, Schumpeter argues that *future values* are requisite. he Schumpeterian conception of value cannot be reduced to preferences and technological production coefficients, as is typical in equilibrium theory. Value is not resolved by an equilibrium equation within a utility-oriented supply and demand system; rather, it signifies the creation of new products, processes, and organizations via strategic decisions and investment.

Consequently, profit assumes a distinct meaning. Rather than functioning as a return to a specific factor, it represents the realization of successful innovation. Furthermore, it forms the source of two categories of (dynamic) costs: prepaid costs for future products manifested as current innovation investments, and deferred costs appearing as balance sheet items for the future implementation of innovations.

Schumpeter thus demonstrates that firms must be organized dynamically. The rules of engagement are not fixed—or at least not permanently so—compelling firms to anticipate or instigate change. This necessitates investment in the future, with a specific focus on innovation and its execution. Innovation is not limited to new products but encompasses the five distinct cases corresponding to the concept of *Implementation of new combinations*, namely (De Jong 1985:57):

1. The production of a good or quality previously unknown to customers or users.
2. The introduction of a production or distribution method not yet practically applied within the relevant industry.
3. The opening of a new market for the specific industry.
4. The conquest or opening of a new source of supply for raw materials and/or semi-finished goods.
5. The implementation of a new organizational form within the industry, whether via merger, acquisition, the dismantling of a monopoly, new distribution models, or a restructured industrial organization.

Schumpeter outlines the existential basis of the firm (based on a specific idea) and the dynamic environment it inhabits. He further specifies the conditions for survival: participation in the perpetual race of creative destruction. However, the internal structuring of these dynamics was not the primary focus of his inquiry. Penrose, in her theory of the firm, gives several theoretical departure points applicable to the core competence concept.

§ 2.2.2 PENROSE'S LEARNING THEORY OF THE FIRM

Penrose shares Schumpeter's critical stance toward equilibrium theories. She argues that in orthodox theory, firm 'growth' is reduced to a mere adjustment in size based on static conditions, ignoring the internal developmental processes that drive cumulative directional shifts. As Penrose observes: *"In that [equilibrium] theory the 'growth' of a firm is nothing more than an increase in the output of given products, and the 'optimum size' of the firm is the lowest point on the average cost curve for its given product; the question what limits the size of a firm is the question what limits the amount it will produce of the given product or products with respect to which the cost and revenue schedules apply that are used to represent the firm. The model is not designed for the analysis of a 'firm' free to vary the kind of products it produces as it grows"* (Penrose 1972:11).

Resources and Productive Services Penrose does not merely examine a firm's output but investigates the entity holistically to explain the drivers of firm growth. In this pursuit, she emphasizes the firm's internal resources, from which *productive services* emanate. It is not the resources per se that form inputs in the production process; rather, the inputs are the services rendered by those resources. *"The services yielded by resources are a function of the way in which they are used - exactly the same resource when used for different purposes or in different ways and in combinations with different amounts of other resources provides a different service or set of services. (…) It is largely in this distinction that we find the source of the uniqueness of each individual firm"* (Penrose 1972:25).

Growth of the Firm Penrose places specific emphasis on the *managerial services* and *entrepreneurial services* that drive firm expansion. The firm is conceptualized as both an administrative organization and a bundle of resources. Managerial services are manifested within the firm's administrative structure, whereas entrepreneurial services include novel concepts regarding products, processes, and organizational forms. The function of managerial services is to integrate these ideas into the existing administrative framework. Once this integration is executed, a surplus of managerial services theoretically emerges, generating renewed impetus for further growth.

This does not imply that a firm can expand indefinitely. In Penrosian parlance, the *inherited managerial resources* dictate the volume of new resources capable of absorption, thereby establishing a fundamental and inevitable constraint on firm expansion at any specific juncture. Should a firm encounter a scenario where expansion outpaces the capacity of individuals to acquire and disseminate new experience and knowledge, the firm will suffer efficiency degradation, irrespective of optimal administrative structural adaptation.

Consequently, the experience and expertise of the managerial cohort play a pivotal role in firm expansion, as the process of experiential acquisition concurrently generates new available productive services. *"The experience gained is…which develops an increasing knowledge of the possibilities for action and the ways in which action can be taken by the group itself, that is, the firm. This increase in knowledge not only causes the productive opportunity of a firm to change in ways unrelated to changes in the environment, but also contributes to the 'uniqueness of the opportunity of each individual firm'"* (Penrose 1972:52–53).

Experience and Knowledge Regarding knowledge and experience, Penrose outlines a critical distinction. The first category is termed *objective knowledge*, which is acquirable from others—essentially, transferable knowledge. The second form, while also the product of a learning process, is grounded in *personal experience*. While experience undeniably yields additional knowledge, it contributes to objective knowledge only to the extent that it is transferable. Furthermore, it must be acknowledged that operational processes and firm expansion are intrinsically linked to the accretion of knowledge and experience. Thus, even absent external stimuli for change (such as market or technological shifts), internal processes generate incremental knowledge that may unveil new productive opportunities. *"Even if the primary purpose is to develop ways of reducing costs and improving the quality of existing products, the exploration and research involved will certainly speed up the production of new knowledge and the creation of new productive services within the firm"* (Penrose 1972:114–115).

In Penrose's conceptualization, a firm represents a collection of resources, and *"…it is the heterogeneity, and not the homogeneity, of the productive services available or potentially available from its resources that gives each firm its unique character"* (Penrose 1972:75). The services generated by resources are contingent upon the individuals utilizing them; conversely, developing those individuals' capabilities depends on the resources employed. This reciprocal interdependence creates the specific productive opportunities unique to a given firm.

For a firm, unused productive services represent *"…at the same time a challenge to innovate, an incentive to expand, and a source of competitive advantage. They facilitate the introduction of new combinations of resources - innovation - within the firm. The new combinations may be combinations of services for the production of new products, new processes for the production of old products, new organization of administrative functions"* (Penrose 1972:85–86).

Penrose resonates strongly with the Schumpeterian process of creative destruction, arguing that *"in a society…the threat of competition from new products, new techniques, new channels of distribution, new ways of influencing consumers demand, is in many ways a more important influence on the conduct of existing producers than any other kind of competition"* (Penrose 1972:113–114). *"In a competitive and technologically progressive industry a firm specializing in given products can maintain its position with respect to those products only if it is able to develop an expertise in technology and marketing sufficient to enable it to keep up with and to participate in the introduction of innovations affecting the products"* (Penrose 1972:132).

A citation elucidating the foundation of the core competence concept states: *"In the long run the profitability, survival and growth of a firm does not depend so much on the efficiency with which it is able to organize the production of even a widely diversified range of products as it does on the ability of the firm to establish one or more wide and relatively impregnable 'bases' from which it can adapt and extend its operations in an uncertain, changing, and competitive world"* (Penrose 1972:137). The alignment with the core competence concept is palpable. In an environment characterized by high uncertainty, rapid technological flux, and abbreviated product life cycles, firms must focus on the development, maintenance, and expansion of their core competencies (bases). These core competencies must yield a diverse array of products perceived by the customer as distinctive. Through this mechanism, firms ensure survival within a Schumpeterian environment.

§ 2.2.3 THE ORGANIZATIONAL ROUTINES OF NELSON & WINTER

Nelson & Winter explain firm behavior—specifically behavioral patterns via the construct of *organizational routines*. These routines are analogous to individual capabilities. The terminology is employed flexibly: "*It may refer to a repetitive pattern of activity in an entire organization, to an individual skill, or, as an adjective, to the smooth uneventful effectiveness of such an organizational or individual performance*" (Nelson & Winter 1982:97). An organizational member may denote an individual or a discrete corporate unit or department. Such a member is competent to execute specific activities independently, possessing a distinct set of capabilities and routines.

This set of capabilities or routines forms the *repertoire*. "*The notion of a hierarchy of organizational routines is the key building block under our concept of core organizational capabilities*" (Nelson 1991:68). The following sections delineate key facets of this conceptual framework.

Routine as Organizational Memory When inquiring into the locus of organizational knowledge storage, the answer ostensibly lies within the organization's memory. However, the precise location of this memory requires definition. Nelson & Winter contend that the routinization of activity represents the primary mechanism for storing organization-specific knowledge; "*...organizations remember by doing*" (1982:99). The underlying premise is that individuals possess specific capabilities retained through enactment. Memory is predominantly realized through practice and resists exhaustive archival in databases or documentation. This assertion does not, however, negate the existence or utility of formal memory repositories.

Sustaining firm routines requires that all members understand their obligations and that these obligations are codified as routines. This necessitates, first, that members possess the requisite routines within their repertoire. Furthermore, members must discern which routines to execute and the appropriate timing for execution. Consequently, each member must possess the capacity to receive and interpret incoming information flows from both internal counterparts and the external environment. The formulation and transmission of accurate information forms the execution of a routine by an organizational member. Therefore, accurate interpretation mandates an awareness of the information's provenance.

The organization is conceptualized as follows: Information flows originating externally are received and interpreted by organizational members, prompting the selection of appropriate routines from their repertoire. Alternatively, resulting from specific actions or targeted communication, members generate information flows directed at other members. These recipients interpret the data and then generate further information flows to other associates, initiating a recursive process. At any given moment, all members are responding to information flows from both the environment and internal sources (*circular flow of information*: Nelson & Winter 1982:103). However, mere possession of requisite routines is insufficient for productivity; coordination is essential. Coordination ensures that each member interprets and transmits information correctly.

Information and knowledge, both articulable and tacit, theoretically reside within the memory of organizational members. However, the relevance of this knowledge depends on context—specifically, the organizational context. This context includes various external memory forms (e.g., databases, reports), the operational environment (e.g., machinery, materials, responsibility structures), and, critically, the knowledge possessed by other members. *"To view organizational memory as reducible to individual member memories is to overlook, or undervalue, the linking of those individual memories by shared experiences in the past, experiences that have established the extremely detailed and specific communication system that underlies routine performance"* (Nelson & Winter 1982:105).

Routine as an Objective: Control, Replication, and Imitation The preceding analysis might suggest that altering routines or deliberately engineering novel, complex routines is difficult. However, routine modification exists along a continuum, ranging from the incremental improvement of existing protocols to radical innovation.

The primary impediment to controlling a routine stems from input differences between firms, even when inputs are nominally identical (e.g., variations in physical dimensions or diverse procurement sources). This variance can be managed through several mechanisms. Inputs may be selected and standardized to satisfy routine specifications; concurrently, the selection process itself may be subjected to control to mitigate error. As a recourse, the routine may be adapted to accommodate available inputs. If systemic failure persists despite these measures, control becomes untenable, potentially causing memory decay. For instance, if a specific member possessing unique knowledge and information departs the firm, a temporal lag inevitably occurs before such knowledge is transferred to a successor. If this transfer proves impossible, the firm suffers not only a loss of organizational memory but potentially the inability to execute the specific routine. This can result in mutations within organizational routines. Because uncontrolled mutations rarely yield improvements within a system of interdependent relationships, organizational control processes are typically designed to suppress such mutations. This dynamic explains the patterned behavior observed in firms.

Regarding replication, Nelson & Winter assert that "*[because the creation of productive organizations is not a matter of implementing fully explicit blueprints by purchasing homogeneous inputs on anonymous markets [(orthodox economic theories)], a firm that is already successful in a given activity is a particular good candidate for being successful with new capacity of the same sort*" (1982:119). Existing routines function as templates and benchmarks. Organizational members must acquire the knowledge embedded in existing routines. Conversely, a firm may seek to imitate the routine of a competitor deemed superior. The critical distinction is that imitation lacks internal transparency regarding the target firm's routines, rendering the process significantly more difficult than internal replication. While reverse engineering is feasible if the routine includes a novel combination of standardized technological elements, it becomes nearly futile if the routine relies heavily on tacit knowledge. In such cases, replication is daunting and imitation nearly impossible, unless the firm resorts to recruiting personnel possessing this tacit knowledge from the competitor.

Routines and Innovation Innovation necessitates the alteration of routines and is characterized by a dual uncertainty. First, there is ambiguity regarding the ultimate form the innovation will take. Second, there is uncertainty concerning the repercussions for existing routines upon implementation.

Innovations originate through diverse pathways. They may emerge endogenously from the standard execution of routine activities; for instance, recurrent failures may reveal opportunities for improvement. Frequently, innovations are derived from the recombination of existing routines (cf. Schumpeter's *implementation of new combinations*).

Even though innovation outcomes are uncertain, the methodology governing the search process is commonly structured; "…*there may also be strong patterns of a highly predictable nature in the [innovation] activity - and to the extend that this is so it seems reasonable to describe the [innovation] activity as 'routinized'*" (Nelson & Winter 1982:132). This implies that while the result remains unpredictable, the trajectory of innovation adheres to identifiable patterns. This aligns with Dosi's concept of technological trajectories, defined as "…*the pattern of 'normal' problem solving activity…on the grounds of a technological paradigm*" (Dosi 1984:15). Consequently, the concept of organizational routines is not antithetical to innovation.

The conceptualization of the organization as a nexus of routines aligns with the core competence framework on several grounds. Fundamentally, it provides an explanation for persistent differences among firms. Firms react to distinct external stimuli, triggering internal consequences. This activates specific routines, which then catalyze the execution of sequential routines. These routines, and more critically their unique combinatorial structures, form the source of inter-firm differentiation. Furthermore, routines provide an opportunity for innovation, whether through the refinement of a single routine or the synthesis of new combinations. "*Competition can be seen as not merely about incentives and pressures to keep prices in line with minimal feasible costs, and to keep firm operating at low costs, but, much more important, about exploring new potentially better ways of doing things*" (Nelson 1991:72).

As Prahalad & Hamel (1990:82) articulate, a core competence represents the collective learning within an organization. This learning is mirrored in the firm's collective memory, a construct that is operationalized through organizational routines. This collective memory encompasses formal archival systems, the physical work environment, and the distributed memory of organizational members. Individual knowledge and memory possess relevance only when integrated with the knowledge and memory of the broader membership, thereby constituting the collective memory.

A final coming together lies in the need of practicing routines. Infrequent performance leads to the atrophy of capabilities—often described as becoming 'rusty'. Knowledge dissipates because its persistence and expansion are contingent upon the execution of routines. This principle applies equally to core competencies: they must be utilized maximally to accrue knowledge and experience. Core competencies that are neglected or underutilized inevitably deteriorate.

§ 2.3 CHARACTERISTICS OF THE CORE COMPETENCE CONCEPT

Teece et al. (1990:19) delineate three critical factors underpinning the core competence concept: *organizational learning*, which helps acquiring new capabilities; *path dependencies*, which direct the focus of the learning process; and the *selection-environment*, which influences the necessity for specific core competencies. Notably, organizational learning and path dependency exhibit interdependence arising from the inside-out orientation of the core competence framework. This approach focus on the leverage of existing knowledge bases (learning), thereby reinforcing path dependencies.

The ensuing analysis of these factors is grounded in the concepts explored in § 1.3 and the theoretical frameworks presented in § 2.2, supplemented by additional relevant theoretical concepts.

§ 2.3.1 ORGANIZATIONAL LEARNING

Porter identifies cumulative learning in an activity as a primary driver of competitive advantage. He notes that *"Performing an activity or a group of linked activities over time creates internal skills and routines which accumulate"* and that *"some skills and routines emerge because of learning over time. This learning is a reflection of past strategy choices which have defined how activities are configured"* (Porter 1991:108–109). This formulation shows the relation between the path-dependent nature of strategy and learning processes. Conversely, Itami emphasizes *learning by doing*, asserting that *"The 'learning by doing' effect enables the firm to accumulate the necessary invisible assets to carry out future strategy in the course of its everyday operations"* (Itami 1987:161). his phenomenon extends beyond production-based experience effects to include the cumulative accumulation of informational assets. Interactions with customers and suppliers generate information flows that augment the firm's internal knowledge base. This may yield enhanced insight into market needs and preferences, refined product design, or augmented problem-solving capabilities. Furthermore, Collis hypothesizes that complex social processes form a potential basis for competitive advantage; these processes are intrinsically linked to organizational learning. He argues that to achieve adaptive and innovative capability, firms must "...*create dynamic routines that facilitate innovation, foster collective learning, and transfer information and skills within the organization*" (1991:52).

Prahalad and Hamel define core competencies as "...*the collective learning in the organization, especially how to coordinate diverse production skills and integrate multiple streams of technologies*" (1990:82). They advocate for the maximal use of these competencies. Unlike physical assets, which depreciate through usage, core competencies appreciate in value as frequent application fosters the accumulation of experience, knowledge, and capabilities via learning processes. While the core capabilities framework historically underemphasizes collective learning, I contend that integrating learning-organization principles is not only feasible but essential. For a capability-based firm to continuously refine business processes in response to evolving customer needs, the cultivation of internal collective learning is need.

Teece et al. argue that the potential for learning is a defining characteristic of economic activity. They describe learning as "...*a process by which repetition and experimentation enables tasks to be performed better and quicker and new product opportunities to be identified*" (1990:19). Penrose extends this logic, asserting that knowledge accumulation "...*also contributes to the 'uniqueness of the opportunity of each individual firm*" (Penrose 1972:53). While individual capabilities are significant, their utility is maximized within the organizational context. A firm may indeed learn through individual knowledge; however, this reliance poses a risk, as the departure of an individual entails the potential loss of that specific knowledge capital.

According to Mills and Friesen (1992), firms may facilitate learning through two alternative mechanisms. The first is the systematization of individual knowledge into formal processes and procedures—essentially, the routinization of knowledge (cf. organizational routines). The second mechanism is the absorption of external entities. This need not imply acquiring an entire firm; it may also encompass the strategic recruitment of individuals possessing specific, high-value knowledge from competitors.

The knowledge and capabilities embedded within organizational routines defy complete codification for intra-organizational transfer. This resistance stems from the fact that complex behaviors within and between routines rely heavily on tacit knowledge, which is inherently inarticulable. Consequently, the routines themselves, alongside management's deployment capability, form the firm's unique capabilities (Teece et al. 1990). This tacit dimension renders such routines inherently difficult to imitate, thereby establishing the firm's distinctive competencies and capabilities. The 'just-in-time' systems employed by many Japanese firms exemplify this phenomenon; despite Western firms understanding the theoretical objective of this routine, successful imitation has remained elusive.

Mills and Friesen (1992) delineate three defining characteristics of a *learning organization*. First, there must be a demonstrable commitment to knowledge, which influences personnel selection and necessitates internal learning mechanisms such as seminars, traineeships, and database management. Second, the firm must possess an internal renewal mechanism, requiring the critical evaluation of routines and the agility to implement necessary changes. Third, the firm must maintain openness to the external environment to ensure responsive adaptability to external shifts.

Senge (1990) introduces the distinctions of adaptive and generative learning, derived respectively from Argyris's (1977) concepts of *single-loop* and *double-loop* learning. The thermostat metaphor aptly illustrates this dichotomy. A thermostat regulates temperature by responding to environmental feedback against a fixed set-point (e.g., 22 degrees); this reactive adjustment exemplifies adaptive learning. Conversely, if the thermostat were capable of interrogating the appropriateness of the 22-degree set-point relative to seasonal contexts, it would be scrutinizing underlying norms rather than merely correcting deviations. This higher-order inquiry forms generative learning. Adaptive learning involves error detection and correction, formal knowledge storage, and environmental response—aligning with the first and third characteristics identified by Mills and Friesen. Their second characteristic, the internal renewal mechanism, aligns with generative learning, which necessitates a paradigm shift and the recognition of the underlying norms governing routines. "*When we fail to grasp the systematic source of problems, we are left to push on symptoms rather than eliminate underlying causes. The best we can ever do is adaptive learning*" (Senge 1990:8). Given the environmental turbulence facing contemporary firms, generative learning—and the velocity of its execution—is increasingly focused on. Standard adaptive processes are insufficient; they are "…*too slow for a world in which the ability to learn faster than competitors may be the only sustainable competitive advantage*" (de Geus 1988:71).

§ 2.3.2 PATH DEPENDENCIES

A logical result of the core competence concept's inside-out orientation is that a firm's existing condition significantly dictates its available strategic options. This dynamic creates consequential implications for the function of strategy. As Itami (1987:2) observes, "*[c]urrent strategy, because it can change the level of invisible 'assets', more than the basis for short-term competitive advantage, it lays the foundation for future strategy and adds to or erodes the invisible asset base*". Strategy content primarily influences the dynamics—specifically, the accumulation and depreciation—of invisible assets. A fundamental hypothesis argued by Collis suggests that a firm's historical evolution acts as a constraint on feasible strategic choices. In operationalizing this hypothesis, he explicitly incorporates the dimension of administrative heritage, thereby outlining the influence of both physical and intangible assets on the firm's choice set.

While Prahalad & Hamel do not explicitly articulate the path-dependent nature of strategy, this characteristic is intrinsic to their argument. For instance, they assert that "…*core competences are built through a process of continuous improvement and enhancement that may span a decade or longer, a company that has failed to invest in core competence building will find it very difficult to enter an emerging market…*" (Prahalad and Hamel 1990:85). This passage underscores a reliance on antecedent investments. Dependence here implies that a firm is perpetually engaged in shaping its future trajectory and potentiality, a process that must form a central tenet of strategy.

Porter similarly demonstrates that firms must contend with market positions established through historical actions. "*The skills and market position a firm has built today are the result of past choices about how to configure activities and what skills to create or acquire*" (Porter 1991:106). While these positions influence strategic choices, Porter argues they are not determinative, as firms retain the agency to reconfigure the value chain. The path-dependent nature of strategy is insufficiently emphasized by Stalk et al. in their explication of the core capability concept; I contend that this aspect warrants greater prominence.

The identification of strategic business processes that generate customer value and defy imitation represents only a partial solution. Sustaining customer value and thwarting imitation necessitates continuous investment in improvements. The establishment of strategic business processes is not a singular event; rather, it depends on the cumulative future investments required to sustain competitive leadership.

Williams (1992) seeks to explain the sustainability of competitive advantage via *isolating mechanisms* (Rumelt 1984), *complementary assets* (Teece 1986), and *organizational routines* (Nelson & Winter 1982). These three partially overlapping factors theoretically create path dependencies—specific patterning within a firm's capabilities. Isolating mechanisms exhibit marked similarities to invisible assets, functioning as latent resources not directly tied to specific products (e.g., robust brand recognition, reputation, and specialized machinery). Complementary assets represent capabilities and assets requisite for prior activities that retain utility for alternative products. Typically situated downstream in the value chain, these assets—such as a product repair facility—often possess cross-functional applicability.

Organizational routines and their inherent preservation tendencies were addressed in § 2.2.3. This list may be augmented by factors identified by Amit & Schoemaker: *scarcity*, *low tradeability*, *durability*, *appropriability*, *limited substitutability*, and *inimitability* (1993:38). These are aspects of resources that influence uniqueness, retention feasibility, and the need for further development, thereby constraining the firm's strategic options. This constraint does not preclude activity modification. While product production and technology use at the SBU level are path-dependent in the short term, the firm level allows greater latitude, permitting novel SBU combinations and acquiring diverse activities, technologies, and capabilities

The concept of path dependency crystallizes the previously discussed path-dependent nature of strategy. *"The notion of path dependencies recognizes that 'history matters'. Thus a firm's previous investments and its repertoire of routines (its 'history') constrains its future behaviour"* (Teece et al. 1990:22). Consequently, learning possibilities are bounded by their relation to antecedent activities. Path dependencies thus delineate adjacent domains where capabilities are most effectively applied. Nelson & Winter identify the neighborhood aspect of search processes for solutions and innovations: *"...the result of today's searches is both a successful new technology and a natural starting place for the searches of tomorrow"* (1982:257). The pursuit and development of new technologies, products, or processes inevitably yields information—often deliberately acquired—that catalyzes subsequent search processes. Logic dictates that solutions be sought in related domains, leading to what Nelson & Winter term *natural trajectories* (1982:258). This constraint is not necessarily negative; it confers the advantage of allowing a firm to successfully transfer existing capabilities to adjacent domains. Through this mechanism, organizational routines and core competencies are perpetuated, sustaining competitive advantage. *"Core business skills need to be constantly exercised to retain corporate fitness"* (Teece 1988:265).

Transaction costs also influence developing new capabilities. Given the path-dependent nature of firm-specific capabilities, they exhibit characteristics analogous to transaction-specific investments. This implies that core competencies involve transaction-specific investments of such magnitude that firms tend to avoid outsourcing associated capabilities, given the heightened risk of opportunism. Consequently, these capabilities are developed internally. Furthermore, internal development gives superior value, allowing for optimal alignment with existing capabilities, productive services, and routines. From a transaction cost perspective, firms will invariably internalize developing capabilities near to their core competencies, a practice that reinforces *path dependency*.

§ 2.3.3 SELECTION-ENVIRONMENT

The conceptual frameworks delineated in § 1.3 devote limited attention to the environmental differences firms encounter. However, Stalk et al. acknowledge that heightened environmental turbulence and complexity amplify the need for core competence thinking.

Preceding sections have examined a Schumpeterian environment, defined by processes of creative destruction that create intense competitive pressure. While such dynamics are prevalent in sectors like computer hardware and consumer electronics, they exert significantly less influence in industries such as agriculture or natural gas. Consequently, a differentiation between distinct environmental typologies appears prudent. Nelson & Winter (1982) allude to the selection-environment of firms and the associated internal search processes. However, this description operates at the meso-level, rendering it insufficiently granular for micro-level firm analysis.

Teece et al. (1990) differentiate between *tight* and *loose* environments. In a loose selection-environment, a firm possesses temporary latitude to adapt to environmental shifts. Conversely, a tight selection-environment precludes such buffer zones, compelling firms to continuously match industry leaders to ensure survival. This study argues that this taxonomy benefits further refinement. Distinctions may be drawn based on the duration of the *resource sustainability cycle* (Williams 1992). Herein, the sustainability of competitive advantage is correlated with the imitability of both the product and firm-specific resources—specifically, the firm's productive services. Williams identifies three resource classes: *slow-cycle*, *standard-cycle*, and *fast-cycle* resources.

Products and services possessing productive service positions insulated from competitive pressure are categorized within the slow-cycle class. In this context, *isolating mechanisms* exert a particularly durable influence; the core competencies underpinning these offerings frequently include patents, geographic advantages, complex buyer/supplier relationships, or established brand equity. Products and services characterized by standardization and suitability for high-volume production reside within the standard-cycle class. Such firms typically exhibit a mass-market and market-share orientation, emphasizing process technology. Productive services in this domain necessitate rigorous control to maintain efficiency at high volumes. Productive services based on a concept, technology, or specific idea belong to the fast-cycle class. These idea-driven products are inherently difficult to shield from imitation. To achieve a dynamic resource fit, these firms require competitive routines aligned with quick time-to-market. Williams outlines several characteristics for each resource cycle regarding market, organization, and strategy (see Figure 2.1).

Williams links the sustainability of competitive advantage to product imitability. If products are easily imitated, competitive advantage proves transient. This is particularly acute in the fast-cycle class. Product imitability, in turn, depends on the imitability of the underlying productive services. Readily imitable productive services inevitably yield easily imitable products. As previously argued, it is necessary for a firm to ensure that its firm-specific resources are resistant to imitation. The proposition holds that when a firm concentrates on its core competencies, the resulting firm-specific resources become difficult to replicate. This study therefore argues that the necessity for core competence thinking intensifies as the resource cycle shortens. This relationship is depicted in Figure 2.1 by the bottom arrow indicating the requisite necessity of core competence thinking.

Figure 2.1

	Class 1	Class 2	Class 3
Market characteristics			
Competitive Analog	Local Monopoly	Traditional Oligopoly	Schumpeterian
Rivalry	Relaxed: sheltered markets, isolated competition	Extended: market share battles, competition on scale	Dramatic: intense rivalry, focus on innovation
Market Scope	Narrow: localized markets	Defined broadly: national or global mass-markets & advertising	Varies: overlaps traditional markets, in state of redefinition
Organizational attributes			
Organizational Analog	Guild-Like	Scale-Orchestrated	Idea-Driven
Economies of Experience	Constrained	Moderate	Supernormal
Control Orientation	Loose	Tight: cost & quality driven	Loose/Tight: (depending on stage of life-cycle)
Strategic priorities			
Critical Success Factors	Nurture protected market & Isolate firm from rivals	Economies of scale Market share/control Buid brand loyalty	Market timing & Intelligence Speed Extract temporary profits
Buyer–Supplier Relations	Stable: Long-term Based on close personal contact	Moderately stable: Brand loyalty vital Emphasis on market share	Unstable: Temporary loyalty Shifting channels of distribution

◀───── Need for Core Competence ─────▶

Source: Williams 1992:42

§ 2.4 CONCLUSION

This chapter demonstrated that the core competence concept cannot be grounded in orthodox economic theories. It has further demonstrated that the core competence concept aligns with alternative economic theories premised on differences between firms and competition derived from those differences. Drawing upon these theories, it is feasible to construct a theoretical framework for the core competence concept.

Three salient characteristics have emerged: *organizational learning, path dependency*, and the *selection-environment*. The first two characteristics underscore the critical importance of acquiring knowledge, capabilities, and experience for a firm centered on its core competencies. The selection-environment characteristic suggests that the need for core competence thinking varies across industries. This need is most pronounced in industries defined by Schumpeterian competition, featuring rapid technological change, easily imitable ideas, and abbreviated product life cycles. In such turbulent environments, identifying stable foundations (core competencies) as the basis for strategy becomes essential.

However, the theoretical framework formulated thus far is insufficient for a more granular understanding of the intra-core competence processes. Furthermore, there is a lack of insight regarding the analytical methodologies required to identify a firm's core competencies. To achieve operational core competence management, such insights are essential. Chapter Three will investigate the feasibility of defining a core competence, the internal processes involved, and the analytical methods for determining a firm's core competencies.

CHAPTER 3: A CLOSER EXAMINATION OF COMPETENCE

This chapter explores the components of a core competence (§ 3.1) and their interrelationships (§ 3.2). Grounded in the theories and concepts examined in Chapters One and Two, these components and their interactions collectively form the definition of a core competence. Additionally, distinct stages of competence maturity are identified and correlated with the selection-environment discussed in § 2.3.3 (§ 3.3). Finally, § 3.4 outlines a methodology for analyzing a firm to identify its core competencies, considering various levels of analysis including end products, business processes, Strategic Business Units (SBUs), and benchmarking.

§ 3.1 THE COMPONENTS OF A CORE COMPETENCE

This section breaks down core competence into several interdependent components. These elements are derived from the definitions of *core competencies*, *resource-based view*, and *core capabilities* as argued by Prahalad and Hamel (1990), Collis (1991), and Stalk et al. (1992), respectively. The selection of these specific concepts is based on their positioning within the *dynamic capabilities* paradigm and the *Strategic Leadership* phase, as established in § 1.1.2.

§ 3.1.1 SYNTHESIS: CORE COMPETENCE, RESOURCE-BASED VIEW, AND CORE CAPABILITY

Prahalad and Hamel argue three criteria a competence must satisfy to be designated as 'core'. First, it must provide potential access to a wide variety of markets. Second, it must contribute significantly to the perceived customer value of the end product. Third, it must be difficult for competitors to imitate. Collis argues that comprehending a firm's strategic decisions requires an examination of its core competencies, organizational capabilities, and administrative heritage. Core competencies are defined as those assets enabling the firm to occupy a unique position. Organizational capability refers to the firm's capacity for continuous improvement in effectiveness and efficiency. Administrative heritage encompasses the legacy assets that constrain current strategic choices. Stalk et al. delineate four principles of competition based on core capabilities. First, corporate strategy is based on business processes rather than end products. Second, success depends on transforming key internal processes into strategic capabilities that deliver superior customer value. Third, firms generate such capabilities by establishing an infrastructure that goes beyond SBU boundaries and integrates diverse functions. Fourth, given the cross-functional nature of these capabilities, strategic leadership is necessarily the domain of top management.

When the criteria from Prahalad and Hamel, Collis, and Stalk et al are viewed in tandem, a cohesive perspective begins to emerge. The concept of core competence suggests that specific internal skills serve as the primary source of end products. As Teece (1982) posits, *"A firm's capability lies upstream from the end product—it lies in a generalizable capability which find a variety of final product applications"*. Consequently, these skills represent a specialized body of knowledge that, when properly cultivated, is inherently difficult to replicate. While end products—patents notwithstanding—are relatively easy for competitors to imitate, the underlying knowledge and skills are tacit and experiential, making them far more resilient to competition. Similarly, the resource-based view identifies core competencies as the drivers of a firm's unique and superior market position. This advantage is multidimensional, spanning various knowledge domains and technical skills; thus, a robust **Knowledge Base** constitutes the first essential component of a core competence.

The definitions of core competence and core capability are fundamentally oriented toward the customer—specifically, the delivery of customer value. This value is defined not merely in monetary terms, but through quality, functionality, and the fulfillment of specific needs. A core competence must contribute significantly to the perceived value of an end-product, and capabilities are deemed 'strategic' only if they are rooted in the customer experience. This is logically consistent: a skill or knowledge set that offers no utility to the end user cannot provide a sustainable competitive advantage. Therefore, **Customer Value** is the second vital component of a core competence.

Stalk et al. emphasize that management plays a pivotal role in this framework. Strategy formulation remains a centralized function of top management, which must establish an infrastructure that transcends SBUs and integrates disparate organizational functions. As Prahalad and Hamel (1990:91) observe, "*[t]op management must add value by enunciating the strategic architecture that guides the competence acquisition process*". This strategic architecture is a managerial responsibility essential for the full utilization of a firm's internal competencies. Similarly, Collis identifies organizational capabilities as a cornerstone of resource-based analysis, noting that successful firms possess the agility to both innovate and adapt to environmental shifts. Consequently, **Managerial Capabilities** constitute the third and final component of core competence.

This tripartite framework aligns with the observation by Prahalad and Hamel (1990:82) that "*[i]f core competence is about harmonizing streams of technology, it is also about organization of work and the delivery of value*".

The tripartite framework raises the question of whether a hierarchy exists among these three components. While a Knowledge Base and Customer Value could theoretically emerge by chance, a sustainable competitive advantage is rarely achieved through serendipity alone. Instead, the cultivation of these elements requires deliberate policy and strategic intent. Because the core competence concept is inherently strategic—focused on the direction and influence of firm resources—this 'capacity to direct' is best embodied by Managerial Capabilities. These capabilities serve a critical linking-pin function, intentionally leveraging and expanding the Knowledge Base to deliver superior Customer Value. While the alignment between knowledge and value may occasionally occur spontaneously, it is the managerial component that ensures this synergy is consistent and goal-oriented.

This perspective aligns with the generally accepted definition of strategic management as "*…a process…and systematic way of relating the company's resources to its environment*" (Steers et al. 1985:489). This study argues that at the core competence level, resources are analogous to the Knowledge Base, while the environment corresponds to Customer Value. At the firm level, resources equate to the firm's core competencies, while the environment encompasses the core competencies of competitors, alongside the broader social, political, economic, and technological context. Consequently, it is argued that Managerial Capabilities are critical for developing the Knowledge Base and maintaining a focus on Customer Value. As the determinant of direction for the other two components, Managerial Capabilities occupy a slightly superordinate position. However, as detailed in § 3.2.4, possessing competence in Managerial Capabilities is a necessary, but not sufficient, condition for the existence of a core competence.

§ 3.1.2 KNOWLEDGE BASE

Nelson and Winter (1982) introduce the concept of *organizational routines*. These routines—and sets thereof, termed *repertoires*—form routinized knowledge (Mills and Friesen 1992), a concept analogous to Penrose's (1972) *productive services*. These routines render each firm unique, as they emerge from the firm's specific experience and knowledge regarding resource management. Consequently, the Knowledge Base extends beyond public, formal, or articulable knowledge, which is relatively common. It encompasses informal knowledge, individual employee expertise, and tacit, non-articulable knowledge. While critical to organizational function, these forms of knowledge are inherently vulnerable. The departure of employees possessing significant tacit knowledge, or the lack of opportunity to deploy such knowledge, depletes the firm's Knowledge Base. Thus, Mills and Friesen (1992) conclude that a firm *learns* when it successfully routinizes individual knowledge and experience, thereby retaining it within the organization.

These routines—in conjunction with the firm's formal records, the work environment, and the routines of other members—form the organizational memory. This collective memory embodies the knowledge and experience of the firm (Nelson & Winter 1982). In a learning organization, individual knowledge and experience are embedded within the firm's routines and productive services. As this knowledge accumulates over time, a concurrent accumulation of routines and productive services occurs via routinization. Through this cumulative process, and particularly through combinatorial effects, the aggregate of routines and productive services goes beyond the sum of its core parts.

The Knowledge Base also functions as the locus for adaptive, or single-loop, learning. Organizational members identify deviations from established norms within their routines and implement corrective changes or improvements. This helps an autonomous development of the Knowledge Base. However, this development is inherently constrained; it evolves from the status quo without examining the underlying concepts (a process reserved for generative or double-loop learning). These foundational concepts encompass the current organizational mode, applied theories, environmental perspectives, and the self-image of the firm and its members. These concepts—or mental models (Senge 1990)—are the (often unconscious) assumptions upon which members predicate their actions when modifying routines. Consequently, these mental models form an integral component of the Knowledge Base.

Accordingly, the Knowledge Base may be conceptualized as follows: Mental models form the structural foundation, serving as the genesis for routines. These routines, in turn, represent the embodied knowledge and experience of the firm. Autonomous modifications and improvements to these routines occur relative to the underlying mental models. Ultimately, the aggregate of these routines forms the firm's memory.

§ 3.1.3 CUSTOMER VALUE

Winter observes that a restaurant patron is rarely interested in the recipe, nor is the consumer purchasing a television typically concerned with the engineering sophistication. *"What is of concern to the customer - and hence should be of intellectual interest of economists - is the ability of organizations to deliver what is wanted"* (1990:272).

While intellectually significant to economists, this concept is of paramount importance to firms. As previously noted, Prahalad and Hamel, along with Stalk et al., emphasize the critical nature of Customer Value regarding end products, processes, and core competencies. An examination of the five dimensions by which capabilities-based firms outperform competitors (Stalk et al. 1990:63) reveals that four are directly correlated with Customer Value: the velocity of response to emerging needs, consistency in meeting expectations, acuity in identifying needs, and the innovation capability to synthesize existing elements into new value propositions. Effectively, the customer determines the validity of core competencies; a competence failing to deliver Customer Value yields no return. Consequently, the firm must align all activities toward the delivery of this value.

Customer Value is generated when a specific product functionality satisfies a distinct customer need. Generally, a product or service possesses a specific functionality that addresses a requirement. For instance, a frozen lasagna gives the functionality of 'prepared food requiring minimal reheating', which satisfies the need for 'time-constrained meal preparation'. Thus, a core competence must be based on the interaction between functionality and need satisfaction. Firms must focus on the continuous upgrading of knowledge and capabilities to produce functionalities that effectively deliver what customers value.

§ 3.1.4 MANAGERIAL CAPABILITIES

Schumpeter discusses *future values*, referring to the creation of new products, processes, and organizations via strategic decision-making and investment. This relates to the concept of *implementation of new combinations*—the recombination of existing elements and routines. Penrose identifies *entrepreneurial services* that are assimilated into the firm by *managerial services*; specifically, the integration of novel productive services into the firm's administrative structure. Nelson and Winter delineate the managerial function regarding the coordination, replication, control, imitation, and innovation of *organizational routines*—the firm's building blocks. As routines and productive services form the source of competencies, they require deliberate management to optimize their use.

While *organizational routines* may emerge spontaneously, deliberate development toward a specific objective requires coordination. Through such coordination, business processes are aligned, enabling members to accurately interpret information flows. This is critical for the proper execution of routines and the associated *circular flow of information* (Nelson & Winter 1982:103). Given that individual members lack a systemic overview of all routines, management assumes a pivotal role. It must identify which routines and productive services are strategic for Customer Value creation and determine which must be replicated or imitated. Management is also responsible for initiating *implementation of new combinations*, thereby transcending innovation within single routines. This process entails the incorporation of new routines, which must be integrated into the aggregate system and aligned with existing protocols.

Senge characterizes this managerial function as the *leader as designer* (1990:10). Management must facilitate and execute generative or double-loop learning. Explicating mental models and subjecting them to critical discourse forms the role of *leader as teacher* (Senge 1990:11), which also entails ensuring that members possess or acquire appropriate capabilities. The *leader as steward* role (Senge 1990:12) primarily entails motivating members and establishing incentives for innovation and adaptive learning. This role determines the firm's openness regarding the environment, significantly influencing informal knowledge acquisition. In this capacity, management can harness informal knowledge acquisition by stimulating its use among members. Furthermore, this role involves aligning members with the firm's objectives (or mission), thereby clarifying the collective goal. This alignment is instrumental in making mental models explicit and facilitating their adjustment.

Knowledge Base, Customer Value, and Managerial Capabilities form the three components of a core competence. The interrelationships between the Knowledge Base, Customer Value, and Managerial Capabilities are examined in the subsequent section.

§ 3.2 DEFINING CORE COMPETENCE

While the three components of a core competence have been delineated, the precise conceptual nature of the concept remains to be clarified. It is proposed that a core competence emerges only when competence exists within all three components and these components interact synergistically— specifically at their intersection. It is possible for competence (but not core) to exist within a single component (e.g., the Knowledge Base) in isolation. In other instances, competencies are characterized by incomplete component interactions - where interaction occurs between two or three of the components.

§ 3.2.1 INTERACTION KNOWLEDGE BASE – MANAGERIAL CAPABILITIES

The concept of organizational routines renders the interaction between the Knowledge Base and Managerial Capabilities distinct. Managerial Capabilities fundamentally entail the coordination and alignment of routines to yield targeted outcomes. This interaction is also evident in processes of replication and imitation. Replication requires identifying routines for duplication, establishing an infrastructure for knowledge transfer, and benchmarking the replicated routine against the original. While organizational members may largely execute these tasks, guidance or supervision is often requisite. Challenges arise particularly when routines include significant tacit knowledge or when members resist knowledge transfer; in such scenarios, management serves an enabling function. Regarding the imitation of third-party routines, a sensing capability is required to identify targets for imitation. Management plays a critical role in determining the mode of imitation (e.g., recruiting personnel from competitors). Furthermore, when attrition creates gaps in the Knowledge Base, management is responsible for remediation, either through internal mechanisms (training) or external acquisition (hiring experts or competitor personnel).

As discussed in § 3.1.4, a critical managerial function is the explication of mental models to facilitate generative learning. For instance, Shell utilizes scenarios and computer models to articulate and intentionally modify mental models (de Geus 1988). In this context, management functions as teacher, facilitator, and catalyst in its interaction with the Knowledge Base. The objective of this interaction is to maximize reciprocal learning, both within the Knowledge Base and within management itself.

Although management must institutionalize an infrastructure (*strategic architecture*) (Zucker 1977) that promotes the frequent use and accumulation of knowledge, the relationship is not unidirectional. Managerial Capabilities are reciprocally influenced by the Knowledge Base. The Knowledge Base provides the informational foundation upon which managerial decisions are predicated; management must consult it to ascertain the feasibility of strategic options. Furthermore, internal developments within the Knowledge Base may prompt managerial decisions to terminate specific routines, initiate new ones, or synthesize novel combinations of routines to drive innovation.

§ 3.2.2 INTERACTION KNOWLEDGE BASE – CUSTOMER VALUE

While this interaction is generally less overt and often less robust, it remains of paramount importance. It functions as the primary conduit for informal knowledge acquisition—a resource often critical to the firm. This interaction typically manifests through routines involving external environmental contact. For example, a sales representative interacting with a client gathers intelligence regarding the firm's products, competitor offerings, and user experiences. This interface also helps adaptive learning, particularly regarding mental models; conceptions of buyers, customers, and suppliers are shaped significantly by these direct empirical interactions.

A prerequisite for this interaction is the openness of routines to environmental information. Without this openness, the firm cannot accurately determine which knowledge is relevant to the desired Customer Value. As Stalk et al. note, acuity in assessing evolving customer needs is a critical dimension of the core competence concept. Beyond adaptive learning regarding mental models, the firm must be capable of learning from discrepancies between internal expectations and market responses. A Knowledge Base calibrated to specific functionalities and Customer Value requires continuous benchmarking against the customer's perception of those attributes. Where divergences exist, the Knowledge Base must adapt effectively. In principle, any element within the Knowledge Base possesses relevance only insofar as it contributes to the creation of Customer Value.

The Knowledge Base influences Customer Value when it generates a value proposition that did not previously exist. This dynamic is also evident in the satisfaction of latent Customer Value, where the value proposition addresses a need that was previously unserved.

§ 3.2.3 INTERACTION MANAGERIAL CAPABILITIES – CUSTOMER VALUE

Within the strategic architecture established and maintained by management, a focus on Customer Value must be institutionalized. This orientation should pervade the entire firm, significantly influencing organizational norms and values. Zucker (1977) concludes that as the degree of institutionalization rises, uniformity regarding constructs such as Customer Value increases, thereby reducing the necessity for direct control mechanisms.

Managerial Capabilities also play a pivotal role in examining mental models regarding Customer Value. While institutionalization implies a collective orientation toward Customer Value, it does not mandate the imposition of a specific, static mental model. Rather, it is the focus on Customer Value that is institutionalized. As mental models evolve, they require periodic re-evaluation. Beyond institutionalizing this focus and facilitating generative learning, management is responsible for identifying which routines are strategic in the context of Customer Value creation.

§ 3.2.4 INTERSECTION OF THE THREE COMPONENTS: CORE COMPETENCE

As argued in the introduction to this section, a core competence resides at the intersection of the Knowledge Base, Customer Value, and Managerial Capabilities—the locus where these three components interact. While a firm may possess competence within a single component, or at the intersection of two, this is insufficient to form a core competence. The following examples—Philips, General Motors, and Van Gelder Papier (detailed in Appendix A)—support this proposition. In each instance, the Knowledge Base, Customer Value, and Managerial Capabilities are analyzed separately. This analytical separation does not fully capture the inherent interdependence of these components.

Philips: Philips was the first to successfully develop a VCR system, with competitors introducing rival systems only four to five years later. This gave a substantial temporal advantage. The firm's ability to pioneer the VCR system indicates a robust Knowledge Base, which theoretically could have been further consolidated while competitors played catch-up. Despite the strategic error of ceding the US market to Japanese competitors—allowing them to accrue substantial experience and refine their technology—Philips succeeded in developing the V-2000 system, a significant technological advancement. The Philips Knowledge Base facilitated this achievement, suggesting the presence of a competence in this domain.

Assessing the presence of Managerial Capabilities is more complex, given the occurrence of several strategic missteps. Market-split agreements proved to be a significant strategic failure; the V-2000's superior image quality was not leveraged effectively due to a lack of features; and acknowledged software issues were left unaddressed despite that Philips' infrastructure did facilitate experimentation and Knowledge Base development. However, absent a demonstrable competence in Managerial Capabilities, at best a neutral role is assumed for the purpose of this analysis.

The critical deficiency for Philips and the V-2000 lay in Customer Value. While the N-1500 was initially successful as an advanced device with unique functionality, the transition to the N-1700 and then the V-2000 was marred by a lack of backward compatibility. This rendered existing tape libraries obsolete—a critical failure from a Customer Value perspective, as consumers lost access to archived content ("memories"). This alienated existing customers, discouraging upgrade purchases and damaged Philips' reputation for customer orientation. Furthermore, the recorders suffered from poor reliability and excessive failure rates. A further technical issue involved the lack of time-based synchronization between Philips recorders and the firm's own televisions, degrading image quality. That Japanese competitors faced similar issues does not mitigate this deficiency.

When a firm focus on Customer Value, compatibility and complementarity with other products and functionalities become paramount. Philips made further critical missteps regarding pre-recorded video tapes. Given that 85% of usage involved viewing pre-recorded content, Philip's extensive programming features failed to address primary consumer needs, whereas content availability would have. Upon recognition of such a misalignment, immediate corrective action is needed. It took Philips however a decade before acquiring the video distributor Super Club and get involved in pre-recorded content.

In the case of the V-2000, the potential to establish a core competence clearly existed, specifically in the domain of magnetic tape audio/video recording and playback. Philips, as the inventor of the compact cassette and the pioneer of the VCR, possessed the requisite Knowledge Base. The failures stemmed primarily from deficiencies in Customer Value and the interaction between Managerial Capabilities and Customer Value. A more rigorous focus on Customer Value would likely have averted failures and ultimate abandonment of the Philip's own VCR system.

General Motors (-1982): Given the American consumer preference for large vehicles—driven in part by low fuel prices—domestic automobile manufacturers focused exclusively on the large, luxury comfort segment. This preference was so deeply entrenched that the small-car segment was neglected, a void successfully exploited by Japanese competitors. It was only when the market share of imported vehicles reached approximately 15% that American manufacturers recognized the necessity for strategic intervention. However, it was primarily the anticipation of rising fuel prices, alongside stricter emission and fuel consumption standards, that compelled General Motors to initiate small-car production.

The existence of Managerial Capabilities at General Motors is demonstrable; it stood as the world's largest automobile manufacturer and, for a significant period, the largest corporation globally. However, scale alone does not form a competence in Managerial Capabilities. Of greater significance was the manner in which General Motors executed the decision to manufacture smaller vehicles. First, it consolidated existing internal knowledge via a Project Centre to meet an 18-month deadline. Additionally, it leveraged foreign knowledge (and routines) already adapted to small-car production. The successful adherence to this deadline—a unique achievement in design duration—evidences a competence in replicating and synthesizing existing routines for new designs. Arguably, General Motors succeeded to some degree in adjusting its mental models, shifting from 'the bigger the better' to 'small can also be beautiful', although the extent of this cognitive shift remains difficult to quantify.

Inherently, these smaller vehicles delivered substantial Customer Value, as evidenced by the rising market share of imported models. Smaller vehicles offer weight reductions and improved fuel efficiency, and yield lower maintenance costs. Furthermore, they offer superior maneuverability in urban environments. Japanese manufacturers successfully demonstrated the viability of this Customer Value proposition within the US market.

General Motors' lack of success with smaller, lighter vehicles is attributable primarily to the absence of the requisite Knowledge Base for their design and production. This deficiency was manifested in a litany of persistent quality issues, ranging from technical failures (e.g., rear suspension failure, chassis corrosion) to safety concerns. Larger, heavier vehicles possess inherent safety advantages due to mass and structural protection in collisions. Smaller vehicles require alternative safety engineering—a domain in which General Motors lacked familiarity. An 86% recall rate over the 1978–1982 period resulted in part from this deficiency, implying that nearly every vehicle sold was returned with defects. In comparison to the 20–35% recall rate of Japanese manufacturers, this figure is exorbitant. Crucially, this rate applied to General Motors' entire small-vehicle fleet. The frequently cited argument regarding Japanese labor cost advantages forms an invalid defense, as Japanese manufacturers later demonstrated the capacity to produce within the US at comparable cost structures.

Despite the presence of Managerial Capabilities and potential Customer Value, General Motors lacked the Knowledge Base required to successfully manufacture smaller vehicles. Had this Knowledge Base been established, the firm could have realized its objective (and potential core competence) to 'supply a car for every purse and every purpose'.

Van Gelder Papier: The tragedy of Van Gelder Papier (Netherlands) is fundamentally a function of power dynamics and the consequent narrowing of perspective among stakeholders—primarily management. Van Gelder Papier achieved great success while holding a monopoly position. However, such positions inherently risk the emergence of—and the fiscal capacity to sustain—organizational arrogance.

This arrogance was manifest in the suppression of wages and the rejection of a US-based paper coating patent with exclusivity for the Dutch market ('not invented here syndrome" in combination with misjudging the magazine market). These issues remained latent until the initial financial losses occurred, becoming critical as losses persisted into the subsequent year. From that juncture, management attempted intervention but without much interaction with the various factories. This isolation likely stemmed from a historical lack of interaction between headquarters and the factories; the corporate center functioned merely as a procurement office.

Applying the core competence components to the Van Gelder case yields the following conclusions. Despite protectionist import tariffs shielding the firm from cheaper foreign competition, a substantial

Knowledge Base must have accumulated over time, evidenced by the inability of domestic competitors to challenge Van Gelder. Further evidence of this Knowledge Base includes the innovation capability of the Apeldoorn and Wapenveld factories when necessity dictated. Delivering Customer Value was not problematic for an extended period, as indicated by the sustained market demand for Van Gelder products.

However, Managerial Capabilities were entirely absent. As noted, interaction between management and the organization was negligible. The central issue was that the factories had acquired excessive power and were unwilling to relinquish it. Consequently, as financial performance deteriorated, management attempted to dismantle this power structure via all available means—initially through 'the accountant', and then through KBB and McKinsey representatives. Even when the NIB representative attempted a constructive approach—achieving positive results for the—this individual was dismissed because the power of the factories wasn't broken. Managerial self-interest (power preservation) superseded the corporate interest. Even during merger considerations, management initially neglected to consult the factories, doing so only after a Supervisory Board member intervened to secure a narrow majority. Ultimately, this internal conflict precipitated the firm's collapse.

The avoidability of this outcome is demonstrated by the post-bankruptcy resurgence of the individual factories. Had management leveraged the factories to generate ideas and enhance coordination, rather than obstructing them, this failure could have been averted. This case illustrates that the possession of a Knowledge Base and Customer Value is insufficient, particularly in the long term, and that Managerial Capabilities form an essential link.

§ 3.3 STAGES OF COMPETENCE

The tripartite framework of Knowledge Base, Customer Value, and Managerial Capabilities helps with the delineation of distinct stages of competence. Four discrete scenarios are identified: the absence of competence in any component, competence in non-overlapping components, competence in overlapping components, and a core competence (defined by the intersection of all three). These stages are illustrated in Figure 3.1 and analyzed in the subsequent subsections. Furthermore, a parallel is drawn between these stages of competence and the selection-environment discussed in § 2.3.3.

Figure 3.1

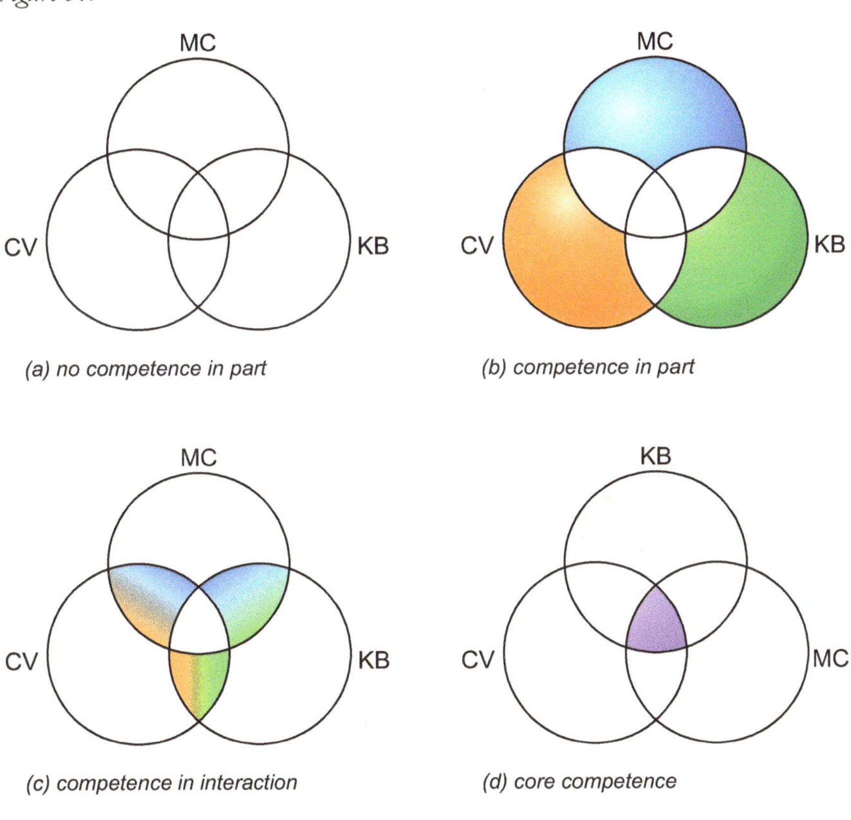

This study argues that the rules of the market within an industry undergo temporal evolution. In certain industries, competitiveness may be sustained via competence in a single component; in others, it necessitates the interaction of two or three components; ultimately, some industries require the possession of fully integrated core competencies. This taxonomy correlates with the classification of resource classes within the selection-environment. Industrial evolution progresses from competition based on isolated component competence, through competition based on interacting components, to competition based on core competencies. This evolutionary trajectory is elaborated below.

§ 3.3.1 NO COMPETENCE IN A COMPONENT

A firm lacking competence in any component (see figure 3.1a) is conceptually untenable. The *raison d'être* of the firm is based on its capacity to deliver value. If there is no Customer Value, a product is unsalable. Furthermore, the delivery of Customer Value typically necessitates a Knowledge Base; in its absence, value creation is severely inhibited. Managerial Capabilities function to align the Knowledge Base with Customer Value. If these foundational elements are absent, the function of Managerial Capabilities is effectively nullified. Moreover, Managerial Capabilities cannot exist as an isolated competence, as they inherently require an object of management.

Consequently, an existing firm must possess competence in at least one domain. This does not imply that such competence necessarily surpasses that of competitors. A firm may persist with mediocre competence; the critical variables are merely the duration and quality of that existence.

§ 3.3.2 COMPETENCE IN NON-OVERLAPPING COMPONENTS

From the preceding analysis, it follows that competence within a singular component (see figure 3.1b) is feasible only regarding the Knowledge Base and Customer Value. Managerial Capabilities are inherently relational and thus cannot exist in isolation. However, possessing competence solely in the Knowledge Base or Customer Value represents an exceptional scenario. Customer Value without a supporting Knowledge Base is sustainable only under conditions of monopoly or extreme scarcity. In such instances, the lack of alternatives prevents the customer from fully assessing the true Customer Value.

A Knowledge Base devoid of Customer Value is frequently observed in subsidized contexts, where the accumulation of specific knowledge is focused despite the absence of attached Customer Value. The case of Japanese Lieutenant Hiroo Onoda, who continued hostilities related to the Second World War until 1974, exemplifies this phenomenon. Onoda defended an isolated Philippine island, dismissing air-dropped repatriation orders as Allied deception. In this instance, the existing Knowledge Base was entirely disconnected from any form of Customer Value or Managerial Capabilities, serving as an extreme archetype (Pile 1979:162). The inherent risk of single-component competence is the obsolescence of either the Knowledge Base or Customer Value. The absence of interaction between components renders the upgrading of competence virtually impossible.

The observation that competition based on non-overlapping components is sustainable only in subsidized or monopoly conditions correlates with the slow-resource cycle class of the selection-environment. Such markets are characterized by local monopolies, where competition is constrained by market protection and isolating mechanisms. Managerial focus on control and efficiency is minimal, with success derived from insulating the firm from potential competitors. The trajectory of Van Gelder Papier prior to its crisis illustrates this state. Critical issues emerged only when the rules of the market shifted (rapid magazine market growth), and competitors began integrating additional core competence components into their competitive strategies. This dynamic is explored further in the subsequent section.

§ 3.3.3 COMPETENCE IN OVERLAPPING COMPONENTS

These scenarios correspond to those detailed in § 3.2.4 (Philips, General Motors, and Van Gelder Papier). In cases of overlapping components (see figure 3.1c), the firm need not possess leading competence in both individual domains. Rather, the competence comes from the interaction between the two—specifically, their alignment and coordination. Here, the synergistic interaction exceeds the sum of the individual component competencies. Consequently, the firm's position is superior to that of a firm possessing only non-overlapping competencies, as the potential for value creation is enhanced.

The environmental context in these instances is best characterized as an oligopoly (the standard-resource cycle class). Competition is driven by market share and economies of scale, with market-scope broadly defined as national or global mass markets. This necessitates a rigorous focus on cost control and quality, requiring enhanced managerial oversight. Critical success factors include economies of scale, market share dominance, and brand loyalty. The market evolution experienced by Van Gelder Papier is illustrative. The competitive landscape shifted with the emergence of a formidable domestic rival, KNP, which focused on delivering Customer Value—specifically through the production of coated paper for the burgeoning magazine market. While Van Gelder Papier remained focused primarily on the Knowledge Base, KNP successfully integrated this Knowledge Base with delivered Customer Value. Subsequent developments demonstrated that this integration had become a prerequisite for competitiveness.

§ 3.3.4 CORE COMPETENCE

A core competence manifests at the intersection of all three components: Knowledge Base, Customer Value, and Managerial Capabilities (see figure 3.1d). Unlike the parallel or sequential interactions characterizing the stage of three separately overlapping components, the interactions defining a core competence are fully integrated. These interactions exert a direct, reciprocal influence upon one another. Consequently, the three components achieve complete alignment, ensuring that development proceeds in a coordinated manner and avoiding the emergence of misalignment.

This necessitates an integrated approach for firms seeking to cultivate core competencies. While it is theoretically possible to construct a core competence sequentially—progressing from competence in a single component, to two overlapping components, to three, and finally to an integrated core competence—this is suboptimal. Given the inherently integrated nature of the construct, it is preferable to first identify the target core competence and then address all three domains simultaneously, with a strategic focus on their integration at the intersection.

Industries requiring this mode of competition are characterized by Schumpeterian pressures and an incessant need for innovation. Within the selection-environment framework, these sectors are classified as fast-resource cycle environments. Contemporary examples include consumer electronics, the computer industry, and telecommunications. In these contexts, market-scope is variable and subject to continuous redefinition. Critical success factors include market timing, intelligence, and velocity; meeting these requirements demands rigorous organizational alignment. NEC exemplifies this approach. In the early 1970s, NEC articulated the strategic objective of developing core competencies in 'Computing and Communication' (C&C). Management identified the necessity of acquiring specific competencies, particularly in semiconductors. A strategic architecture was established wherein senior management analyzed the trajectory of various competencies and products, while strategic alliances were leveraged to secure essential technologies. This strategic intent was communicated internally and clearly articulated to external stakeholders. Furthermore, cross-functional and trans-SBU 'coordination groups' were instituted. The C&C strategy targeted the anticipated coming together of computing, communication, and components. A firm capable of serving this nexus would command significant opportunity. This coming together was expected to manifest in customer preferences and demand for integrated products, such as videophone systems and facsimile machines.

Consequently, NEC pursued simultaneous development across all three components. It established a strategic architecture via SBU-crossing coordination groups, expanded its Knowledge Base through strategic alliances, and oriented its focus toward Customer Value regarding the integration of computing and communication. NEC remains the only firm ranked among the top five globally in telecommunications, semiconductors, and mainframes—a testament to the efficacy of core competence theory and management.

§ 3.4 ANALYSIS OF A FIRM'S CORE COMPETENCIES

The immediate analytical challenge concerns the methodology for identifying a firm's core competencies, provided they exist. The difficulty lies in the fact that core competencies are not concrete products but abstract, general capabilities that typically transcend individual SBUs. One potential solution is the examination of business processes, as advocated by the core capability concept. Furthermore, identifying a competence requires comparative analysis against competitors. Theoretically, a competence is valid only if it is unique and superior relative to the competition.

However, a firm need not necessarily excel in a single component, such as the Knowledge Base, to possess a unique competence. Superiority may instead derive from robust interactions, such as those between Managerial Capabilities and Customer Value. The following subsections review analytical possibilities at various levels of the organization.

§ 3.4.1 LEVEL OF ANALYSIS: END PRODUCTS

End products form the firm's revenue generators. In the frameworks of Ansoff and Porter, competition occurs primarily at this level, with competitive advantage achieved via cost leadership or differentiation. Although core competence theory adopts an internal perspective, end products may be viewed as the manifestation of higher-level competencies. This implies a causal relationship between end products and firm competencies. Theoretically, therefore, it should be possible to trace a firm's competencies through an analysis of its end products.

However, end product success may be a by-product, resulting from external factors such as a high-growth market. In such scenarios, competitive pressure is low, as the primary need is satisfying abundant demand. Later, as the market saturates and competition intensifies, the firm may fail due to the revelation of underlying competence deficiencies.

This presents a potential analytical challenge when attempting to identify competencies via end products. If this approach is employed, the focus must shift from similar products or product categories to the functionality these products provide and the specific needs they satisfy. The interplay between functionality and need satisfaction is critical regarding the delivery of Customer Value.

§ 3.4.2 LEVEL OF ANALYSIS: BUSINESS PROCESSES

Stalk et al. (1992) take business processes as the primary unit of analysis. They argue that strategy must be based on business processes. Such processes are deemed strategic when they deliver Customer Value; furthermore, extended chains of strategic business processes impede competitive imitation.

When adopting business processes as the analytical baseline, the underlying concept demands scrutiny. One must determine the purpose of the process and its functional relationship to other processes. Such an examination explains the firm's organizational routines, which, in turn, reveal the underlying Knowledge Base.

§ 3.4.3 LEVEL OF ANALYSIS: CORPORATE AND SBU LEVELS

An SBU represents a specific product/market combination. Prahalad & Hamel (1990) critique the *"tyranny of SBU thinking"*, arguing that SBUs hoard firm resources and capabilities. However, in the analysis of competencies, evaluating the positive attributes of SBUs has value. For instance, one might examine the support activities an SBU performs for its products. An internal infrastructure may exist within an SBU that enhances its operational efficacy. Conversely, competencies typically transcend SBU boundaries, requiring analysis at the corporate level. Here, too, an infrastructure may exist that benefits both SBUs and potential competencies. The analytical focus must be on cross-SBU infrastructure, extending beyond mere staff functions. These infrastructures, at both SBU and corporate levels, offer insight into the firm's Managerial Capabilities.

§ 3.4.4 LEVEL OF ANALYSIS: BENCHMARKING

The question "when is a competence a competence?" implies that a competence exists only when it surpasses that of competitors—a comparison termed benchmarking. As previously established, a firm need not excel in every individual core competence component; rather, the interaction between components is paramount, as this nexus generates added value.

This perspective permits two modes of competitive comparison: first, benchmarking individual core competence components against those of competitors; second, comparing the internal interactions of components within the firm against analogous interactions within competitor firms.

A significant impediment involves obtaining insight into competitors' relevant components. While Customer Value is relatively ascertainable, Managerial Capabilities and, specifically, the Knowledge Base present substantial investigative challenges. Determining the interactions between core competence components is likely even more challenging. Nonetheless, the endeavor remains a valuable exercise.

§ 3.4.5 INTEGRATION OF THE LEVELS OF ANALYSIS

As deduced from the preceding subsections, these levels of analysis facilitate the examination of Customer Value, Managerial Capabilities, and the Knowledge Base, respectively. Analyzing end products in terms of functionality and need satisfaction illuminates the Customer Value delivered. Examining infrastructure at corporate and SBU levels identifies potential Managerial Capabilities. Finally, analyzing business processes reveals the firm's organizational routines and, consequently, its existing Knowledge Base.

Furthermore, each component allows for competitive benchmarking—individually, in terms of interaction, and at the aggregate level of the core competence. A methodology for determining core competencies is delineated in Figure 3.2.

Figure 3.2

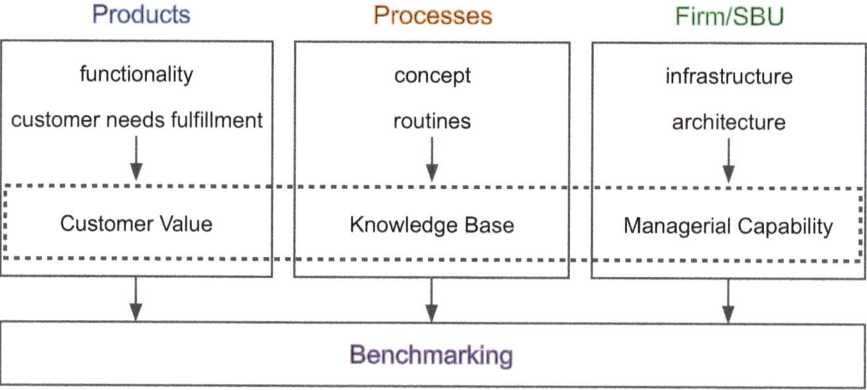

§ 3.5 CONCLUSION

Drawing upon the theories of Schumpeter, Penrose, Nelson & Winter, Prahalad & Hamel, Collis, and Stalk et al. discussed in Chapter Two, the components of a core competence have been identified: Knowledge Base, Customer Value, and Managerial Capabilities It is the interaction among these components that generates the competitive advantage dynamics of a core competence.

An analytical methodology for identifying a firm's core competencies has been presented. This approach entails examining a firm's end products to ascertain sources of Customer Value; analyzing internal business processes to uncover the underlying Knowledge Base; and assessing cross–SBU infrastructure to identify Managerial Capabilities. These dimensions are subsequently benchmarked against those of competitors to delineate core competencies.

Clearly, a core competence is a complex phenomenon, raising the question of how such processes can be directed. Given this complexity, developing a specific organizational structure that fully accommodates core competence management is likely unfeasible. Instead, it requires a managerial framework and a representation of the requisite internal processes. The subsequent chapter will examine the utility of cybernetic and holographic organizing principles for this purpose.

CHAPTER 4: ORGANIZATIONAL IMPLICATIONS

Thus far, the discourse has addressed the origins, foundations, and functional mechanics of the *core competence* concept. This chapter examines the implications of 'core competence management,' outlining the internal processes required for the full realization of core competencies.

The inquiry first identifies streams within the organizational literature and advances the argument that these align closely with systems theory. Subsequently, the influence of applicable organizational principles on core competencies will be considered, specifically regarding the Knowledge Base, Customer Value, and Managerial Capabilities. This is followed by an analysis of processes at the sector and national levels (Best 1990; Porter 1990). Both authors describe mechanisms for upgrading knowledge and resources within a sector; these processes warrant comparison with the dynamics of core competence management.

§ 4.1 APPROACHES TO ORGANIZATIONS

In *Organization Theory* (1983), Bryans & Cronin delineate roughly three streams within organizational literature: classical organization theory, human relations theory, and systems theory. These three streams are briefly discussed in the subsequent subsection, concluding that core competence management aligns most robustly with systems theory. Subsequently, within the framework of systems theory, cybernetic and holographic organizing principles are examined (Morgan 1986), as they exhibit strong conceptual affinities with core competence principles. Here, the organization is analogized to the brain, reflecting its potent self-organizing capabilities.

§ 4.1.1 STREAMS WITHIN THE ORGANIZATIONAL LITERATURE

Classical Organization Theory At the turn of the century, various conceptual frameworks emerged to manage the larger, more complex organizations spawned by the industrial revolution. These concepts have exerted, and continue to exert, a major influence on organizational theory.

They can be categorized into three distinct blocs: scientific management, formal organization theory, and bureaucracy.

Scientific management derives from Taylor's principles, which provided guidelines for controlling and coordinating tasks to enhance efficiency. This approach was based on hierarchical structures and specialization, extending to time-motion studies designed to determine optimal task execution times for production maximization. This resulted in a mechanistic and economic conception of the human agent—a micro-level approach to shop-floor optimization.

Formal organization theory and bureaucracy employ a macro-level approach. Fayol, the originator of formal organization theory, argued that efficiency is maximized through the application of universal principles. These include specialization, top-down authority, unity of command, span of control, vertical communication, and the separation of line and staff. The emphasis is predominantly structural, with little regard for the sociological and psychological dimensions of the workforce.

Bureaucracy stems from the theories of sociologist Max Weber. The central organizing principle is that rational-legal authority is recognized by employees based on the manager's hierarchical position. While sharing several principles with formal organization theory, bureaucracy places specific emphasis on rules and procedures.

These three classical theories share an emphasis on formal organization and the bifurcation of conception (thinking) and execution (doing). In contrast, core competence logic is based on the integration of conception and execution, as this synthesis generates opportunities for learning, experience accumulation, and capability expansion. Excessive emphasis on formal structure impedes the novel deployment of these experiences and capabilities. Furthermore, classical organization theory is strictly internally oriented, neglecting environmental contexts. Conversely, core competence thinking incorporates these contexts through Customer Value, formal and informal environmental knowledge acquisition, and technological developments.

Human Relations Theory Human relations theory is typically associated with the Hawthorne studies, which demonstrated that productivity relies on factors beyond wages, management layers, and the physical work environment. The firm is also a social system comprising informal organization, motivation, morale, communication, and group dynamics. The primary conclusion was that productivity correlates arguably with the satisfaction of individual employee needs.

Critiques of this theory primarily target its neglect of the firm's multifaceted nature, specifically the roles of technology and the environment. From a core competence perspective, this omission is critical. While core competence thinking acknowledges the psychological and sociological dimensions of the workforce, it regards technology and environmental influences as indispensable—evident, for instance, in the role of technology within the Knowledge Base and the delivery of Customer Value to the environment.

Systems Theory Systems theory attempts to improve this deficiency by arguing that a firm includes distinct subsystems (sociological, technological, economic, structural) which, while autonomous, are fundamentally interdependent. System optimization requires the inclusion of all subsystems in the analysis. This establishes a conceptual framework for understanding interactions among components. Crucially, while the firm is viewed as a composite of subsystems, the system as a whole is understood to be greater than the sum of its parts.

Systems are categorized as either closed or open. A closed system possesses rigid boundaries that restrict environmental interaction. Conversely, a firm is generally conceptualized as an open system engaged in dynamic interaction with its environment. To maintain equilibrium, the firm must continuously adapt within and between its subsystems. This adaptation varies across firms, as each operates within unique contexts (contingency approach).

Critiques of systems theory primarily target the phenomenon of reification, wherein the firm is anthropomorphized as an autonomous agent possessing a distinct personality and capacity for action, rather than conceptualized as an aggregate of individual actors. I concur with this critique; referencing 'the organization' as a singular entity risks obscuring the multifaceted nature of organizing processes. However, for the purposes of conceptual modeling, distinguishing between the organization and its environment retains practical utility, despite the porosity of the boundary separating them. Consequently, references herein to 'the organization' and 'the environment' are employed for conceptual clarity, with the understanding that the internal psychological and social contexts remain integral to the analysis.

In my assessment, core competence thinking aligns most robustly with systems theory. It recognizes the individual and social aspects of organization regarding learning processes, experience, and capabilities, while simultaneously according significant weight to economic and environmental factors such as technology, Customer Value, and the Knowledge Base. The core competence model presented in Chapter Three forms a system in its own right, comprising three interacting subsystems where the aggregate exceeds the sum of the components.

Systems theory as outlined here provides insufficient scaffolding to fully operationalize core competence management. Consequently, the subsequent subsection elaborates on *cybernetic* and *holographic* organizing principles derived from systems theory.

§ 4.1.2 CYBERNETIC AND HOLOGRAPHIC ORGANIZING PRINCIPLES

Cybernetic Organizing Principles Cybernetics forms an interdisciplinary field dedicated to the study of information, communication, and control. Etymologically derived from the Greek *kubernetes* ('helmsman'), the discipline characterizes the processes through which machines and organisms demonstrate self-regulating behavior. Its initial objective was developing machines capable of mimicking the adaptive capacities of biological organisms, specifically the self-organizing faculties of the brain.

A seminal conclusion of this field argues that a system's capacity for self-regulation depends on information exchange characterized by negative feedback. Negative feedback mechanisms operate via error detection and automatic correction: deviations exceeding a specified threshold trigger countervailing movements to maintain a desired trajectory. *"Cybernetics shows us that organized forms do not actively seek or orient themselves toward achievement of a desired future state. Rather, they arrive at any given state through processes of adjustment which eliminate other possible system states"* (Morgan 1983:347).

This principle is explained by the act of grasping an object. Intuitively, one assumes the hand, guided by visual supervision, advances directly toward the target. Cybernetics gives an alternative interpretation. The act of grasping is a continuous process of deviation elimination, wherein the spatial disparity between hand and object is progressively reduced until the deviation is nullified. Effectively, one grasps an object by avoiding the state of not grasping it. This process corresponds to the adaptive, or single-loop, learning discussed in preceding chapters. Cybernetics outlines four assumptions for communication and learning (Morgan 1986:86–87). First, systems require sensory capabilities to detect significant environmental variables. Second, they must possess the capacity to correlate this information with established behavioral norms. Third, the system must be capable of detecting deviations from these norms. Fourth, mechanisms must be in place to generate corrective action upon the detection of discrepancies. The fulfillment of these four conditions establishes a continuous information exchange between system and environment, enabling perception of change and appropriate response—thereby manifesting self-regulating behavior.

This mechanism functions effectively provided the behavioral norms remain aligned with environmental conditions. However, when this alignment fractures, negative feedback yields actions that are inadequate due to the obsolescence of the governing norms. Consequently, cybernetics differentiates between learning and *"learning to learn"*—specifically, the distinction between single-loop and double-loop learning. Double-loop learning represents the capacity to examine the relevance of underlying behavioral norms and to adjust them as necessary.

While the principle of single-loop learning is institutionalized in many firms—most notably in budgeting processes—the capacity for double-loop learning is significantly rarer. Morgan (1986:89–90) identifies three structural barriers to its adoption. The first is the inherent nature of bureaucratic organizations, which impose fragmented cognitive patterns and discourage independent thought. Corporate objectives and structures are cascaded to lower levels as isolated responsibilities. Consequently, personnel at these levels frequently lack a holistic perspective or a clear understanding of their operational context. A second barrier stems from bureaucratic accountability. Employees operate within incentive structures that reward success and penalize failure, thereby fostering the concealment of errors or the avoidance of problem identification to mitigate personal risk. Alternatively, problems may only be acknowledged when solutions are pre-identified. A third barrier arises from the dissonance between what people say and what they do (often unconscious). This frequently results in scenarios where problems are ostensibly approached with rationality to project competence. However, should the situation threaten an individual's position, the response often shifts to attribution of blame and the intensification of standard operating procedures.

The process of double-loop learning is based on openness to environmental flux and a willingness to fundamentally examine underlying behavioral assumptions. Morgan gives four guidelines for cultivating double-loop learning processes (1986:91–95): 1. Cultivate a culture that valorizes the acceptance of error and frames uncertainty as an intrinsic component of a complex, dynamic environment. This helps a constructive engagement with uncertainty. 2. Promote a multidisciplinary approach to complex problem-solving. This ensures problems are examined from diverse perspectives, fostering developing more creative and comprehensive solutions. 3. Eschew the imposition of rigid action structures. *"Whereas the traditional philosophy is to produce a master plan with clear-cut targets, cybernetics suggests that it may be systemically wiser to focus on defining and challenging constraints"* (Morgan 1986:92). Strategy thus shifts from selecting end-goals to defining constraints (the negative feedback boundaries to be avoided). This approach finds a parallel in the Japanese *ringi* decision-making process. 4. Execute structural interventions to establish organizational frameworks that ensure the implementation and continuous maintenance of these principles.

This final principle segues into the holographic approach to organization, offering insights into the capabilities required for an organization to emulate the flexible, self-organizing nature of the brain.

Holographic Organizing Principles In *Images of Organization*, Morgan (1986) employs the metaphor of the brain to explain holographic organizing principles. A hologram is a photographic record wherein interacting light beams generate an interference pattern captured on a plate. Upon illumination, the original image is reconstructed. A salient characteristic of a hologram is its distributive nature; if fragmented, each individual segment retains the capacity to reproduce the entire image. The whole is thus encoded within the parts. It is hypothesized that neural architecture functions analogously. This is exemplified by maze-navigation experiments with rats, where the removal of up to ninety percent of the brain (sparing the visual cortex) did not significantly impede navigational capability. Similarly, substantial portions of the motor cortex may be excised without inducing paralysis, resulting merely in a degradation of motor performance.

The holographic nature of the brain is principally manifested in the dense interconnectivity of neurons, each linking to hundreds or thousands of others, creating a system that is simultaneously generalist and specialized. While distinct neural regions possess functional specialization, they do not exercise exclusive control or autonomous execution. The neural network is highly distributed, allowing specific components to substitute for others. Consequently, the whole is resident within the parts, and connectivity and substitution supersede structural differentiation.

A further dimension of this interconnectedness is a latent exchange capacity that remains largely dormant until activated. This surplus is foundational to the system's holographic potential and operational flexibility. *"The redundancy allows the brain to operate in a probabilistic rather than a deterministic manner, allows considerable room to accommodate random error, and creates an excess capacity that allows new activities and functions to develop"* (Morgan 1986:96). This redundancy is the base for self-organization, permitting the co-evolution of internal structures and functional outputs in response to environmental fluctuations.

Morgan concludes that establishing a holographic organization necessitates the following: get the whole into the parts, create connectivity and redundancy, create simultaneous specialization and generalization and create a capacity to self-organize (Morgan 1986:95–96). He integrates these prerequisites with four interacting holographic principles: *redundancy of functions, requisite variety, learning to learn,* and *minimum critical specification.* These principles are illustrated in Figure 4.1.

Figure 4.1

Source: Morgan 1986:90

The principle of redundancy of functions entails embedding the whole within the parts via redundancy, thereby generating simultaneous specialization and generalization. Conceptually, two distinct ways exist for introducing redundancy into a system. The first is redundancy of parts, wherein each component is designed for a specific function. Supplementary parts are introduced for control and as backups in the event of failure. This forms a mechanistic approach, typically resulting in a hierarchical structure where specific units control others. The second method is redundancy of functions. Rather than adding parts, additional functions are integrated into existing components, engaging each part in a spectrum of activities beyond a single specialization. Systems based on functional redundancy exhibit holographic properties, as capabilities relevant to the entire system are embedded within individual components. This establishes a novel relationship between the part and the whole.

A critical question concerns the optimal magnitude of redundancy to be embedded within a specific part. Here, the principle of requisite variety is paramount. Ashby (1958) argues that the internal diversity of a self-regulating system must match the variety and complexity of its environment to effectively navigate environmental change. "*…the variety in the outcomes [E], if minimal, can be decreased further only by a corresponding increase in that of R [regulatory system]. This is the law of requisite variety. To put it more picturesquely: only variety in R can force down the variety due to D [environmental variation]; only variety can destroy variety*" (p.207). (for mathematical proof, see Appendix B). This implies that redundancy must be embedded at the point of need, rather than elsewhere.

The principles of redundancy of functions and requisite variety create the capacity for systemic self-organization. To actualize this capacity and ensure coherent directionality, the remaining two principles are essential. Minimum critical specification inverts the bureaucratic need that organizational arrangements be defined with maximal specificity. Such rigidity precludes self-organization. Conversely, minimum critical specification argues that management should function primarily as a facilitator, establishing enabling conditions that allow the system to self-structure. "*The minimum conditions are what might be understood as 'enabling conditions' - conditions that enable a system to initiate key processes necessary for its continued existence*" (Morgan 1983:7). This approach preserves flexibility by specifying only the absolute essentials required for activity execution. However, the potential for entropy persists. Consequently, the fourth principle, *learning to learn* (double-loop learning), is requisite. As previously noted, self-regulating systems require double-loop learning to maintain a coherent normative framework against which to calibrate responses to environmental flux.

This study argues that these holographic principles demonstrate significant alignment with core competence management. They reiterate the criticality of double-loop (or generative) learning within the Knowledge Base and Managerial Capabilities; they conceptualize the firm as an open system capable of delivering appropriate Customer Value through redundancy and requisite variety; and they offer strategic guidelines for Managerial Capabilities. The specific relationship between these holographic principles and the Knowledge Base, Customer Value, and Managerial Capabilities is examined in the subsequent section.

§ 4.2 HOLOGRAPHY AND CORE COMPETENCE

This section examines the implications and potential applications of holographic organizing principles regarding the tripartite framework of core competence components: Knowledge Base, Customer Value, and Managerial Capabilities.

§ 4.2.1 REDUNDANCY OF FUNCTIONS AND CORE COMPETENCE

Section 3.1.2 explained the Knowledge Base and the role of organizational routines as repositories of knowledge. Nelson & Winter (1982) introduce the concept of *repertoires*—sets of organizational routines performable by an individual member. This concept shows strong theoretical alignment with the holographic principle of functional redundancy. Augmenting member repertoires with additional routines fosters organizational flexibility through simultaneous generalization and specialization. Consequently, members can execute routines on behalf of others, creating a more holistic comprehension of the system. While embedding a critical mass of routines allows the whole to be substantially represented within the parts, this process is constrained by the finite cognitive capacity of individuals and groups to master extensive routine sets.

Regarding Customer Value, redundancy of functions is situated primarily within routines directly associated with value delivery. High redundancy is requisite here; ideally, every organizational member should possess repertoire routines directly linked to Customer Value. This widespread use fosters universal member engagement with the customer and the value proposition. Furthermore, direct interface helps information exchange, thereby amplifying opportunities for both single-loop and double-loop learning.

Regarding Managerial Capabilities, redundancy targets the cultivation of self-organizing capacities among members. Consequently, Managerial Capabilities must be embedded within individual repertoires. This proposition appears theoretically at odds with the assertions of Prahalad and Hamel (1990) and Stalk et al. (1992), who contend that strategic direction resides exclusively with top management. However, this apparent contradiction allows for reinterpretation. Top management should primarily assume the roles of *teacher* and *steward* (Senge 1990), while devolving the role of *designer* to lower organizational levels. Consequently, the function of Managerial Capabilities shifts toward facilitation—establishing the preconditions and parameters within which members can generate their own designs. The focus is on provisioning an infrastructure (*strategic architecture*:

Prahalad and Hamel 1990) rather than imposing rigid structures and tasks, which invariably stifle flexibility and creativity.

§ 4.2.2 REQUISITE VARIETY AND CORE COMPETENCE

The requisite degree of redundancy within *repertoires* is determined by the level of exposure to environmental variety; essentially, redundancy must be situated where immediate need exists. Since the Knowledge Base theoretically encompasses all the firm's routines—from sanitation to R&D—the firm must absorb every form of environmental variety relevant to those routines. Given potential cognitive overload, it may be prudent to revert to core competence and capability frameworks, categorizing the Knowledge Base into knowledge domains and strategic processes. This taxonomy helps the targeted absorption of environmental variety into the Knowledge Base, specifically where it is most critical.

Regarding the requisite variety of Customer Value, the analytical focus must rest on the diversity of functionality and customer need satisfaction. Since Customer Value is based on the interaction between functionality and satisfaction, all forms of environmental variety are significant and must be integrated where directly relevant. This ensures the capacity to detect and respond appropriately to shifting customer preferences.

The magnitude of redundancy within Managerial Capabilities depends on two criteria. First, sufficient redundancy is necessary to create self-organizing capacity among members. Second, the firm must function as an open system to perceive and assimilate environmental variety. Therefore, Managerial Capabilities oriented toward environmental openness must exist in redundant form to prevent excessive internal focus and subsequent blindness to environmental shifts.

§ 4.2.3 MINIMUM CRITICAL SPECIFICATION AND CORE COMPETENCE

The principle of minimum critical specification entails creating facilitating conditions that enable self-organizing behavior. For the Knowledge Base, this mandates that members possess or acquire the minimum knowledge and capabilities requisite for routine execution. This has implications for recruitment, information exchange, and continuous education. Furthermore, an environment must exist where knowledge and capabilities can be deployed for experimentation without penalizing individuals for resulting errors or failures. As detailed then, such errors are pedagogical inputs, preventing chaos. The aggregation of diverse perspectives is also a critical condition for the Knowledge Base, facilitating multidisciplinary problem-solving and comprehensive solution development.

With respect to customer value, it is necessary that all members are actively engaged in value delivery and possess the required capabilities. Members must be cognizant of the functionality of produced goods and services and the specific needs they satisfy. Optimal Customer Value delivery depends on this universal focus. Consequently, conditions must facilitate the rapid detection of evolving customer needs, permit diverse approaches to satisfaction, and provide latitude for rapid innovation and combinatorial novelty.

Evidently, minimum critical specification is predominantly a core of Managerial Capabilities. These capabilities must construct an infrastructure wherein minimum critical specification is embedded. Only through such an infrastructure will the flexibility of self-organizing members materialize. The specific configuration of this infrastructure will vary across firms. History demonstrates there is no single 'best way' to organize. Consequently, Managerial Capabilities are themselves subject to minimum critical specification. No singular (infra)structure can be imposed as universally correct. The minimum critical specification for Managerial Capabilities is, minimum critical specification itself.

§ 4.2.4 LEARNING TO LEARN AND CORE COMPETENCE

Within the Knowledge Base, accommodation must be made not only for single-loop (adaptive) learning but also for double-loop (generative) learning. This occurs primarily through interaction with Managerial Capabilities, which ensure that the underlying assumptions governing behavioral patterns (*mental models*) are continuously scrutinized for validity. This scrutiny is critical for facilitating appropriate behavioral adaptation. Furthermore, learning derived from errors and failure is instrumental in establishing a more coherent behavioral trajectory.

This principle is equally critical regarding Customer Value. Sustaining the delivery of appropriate and sufficient Customer Value necessitates continuous customer interaction and a receptivity to learning from these exchanges. *Mental models* concerning the customer and value propositions must go through continuous adjustment. Otherwise, the firm risks entrenchment in obsolete dogmas regarding clientele, needs, and value delivery.

Managerial Capabilities bear the responsibility for governing double-loop learning processes. They must define minimal conditions to foster the organic emergence of these processes, eschewing the imposition of rigid procedures or structures. Acknowledging the absence of a singular one best way of organizing, Managerial Capabilities must themselves actively engage in double-loop learning. Lessons must be extracted from errors, and the assumption of finality during periods of success must be avoided. Stagnation effectively forms decline. Core competence management and holographic organizing represent continuous, ceaseless cycles.

In this section, holographic organizing principles have been addressed individually. However, as previously indicated, these principles—like the components of core—are fundamentally interdependent. Consequently, the aggregate reality is significantly more complex than this representation suggests. While a systematic list of all interdependencies is unfeasible, this stylized representation serves to explain specific points of intersection between the organizing principles and core competence components.

§ 4.3 HOLOGRAPHIC PRINCIPLES IN SECTOR AND COUNTRY PROCESSES

This section reviews the theories of Best (1990) and Porter (1990, both of whom identify holographic-like processes at the level of the industrial sector and the country of origin, respectively. Both theories demonstrate that the country of origin and its internal sectors are critical for developing core firms; specifically, a cluster is superior to the individual firm in upgrading knowledge, capabilities, resources, and productivity. This advantage is realized through processes of cooperation and competition. These theories further indicate a growing emphasis on the inside-out approach. Conceptually, they may be viewed as macro-level core competence theories, as they are based on knowledge, experience, capabilities, and upgrade potential. However, the level of analysis shifts from the firm to the superordinate environment. Because these theories describe processes analogous to those previously discussed, they are briefly reviewed here to demonstrate the applicability of holographic organizing principles across different levels of analysis. The analysis commences with Best, who argues that clustered firms should focus on collaboration over price-based attrition. Rather than competing toward mutual exhaustion, firms should engage in Schumpeterian competition, focusing on product and service innovation. Next, the analysis addresses Porter, who argues that intense competition—including price rivalry—within a cluster ultimately benefits individual firms by fortifying their long-term competitive advantage relative to external peers.

§ 4.3.1 BEST: THE NEW COMPETITION

In the introduction to *The New Competition: Institutions of Industrial Restructuring*, Best outlines a paradigm shift in competition: from *price-led* to *product-led* competition. The contemporary objective is not price minimization but the manufacture of superior products that satisfy customer requirements. Best identifies the entrepreneurial firm as the foundation of this competitive form, defining it as "*...an enterprise that is organized from top to bottom to persue continuous improvement in methods, products and processes*" (1990:2). Best distinguishes four dimensions of this new competition:

1. **The Firm: The Collective Entrepreneur** The primary attribute of the entrepreneurial firm is its strategic orientation. The firm actively selects its competitive domain rather than accepting it as a given. A second attribute is the organizational objective; "*...the goal of the entrepreneurial firm is to gain strategic advantage by continuous improvement in process and product*" (1990:11–12). A third attribute pertains to the organization of production. The pursuit of continuous improvement to achieve superior product performance necessitates continuous problem solving. Consequently, the entrepreneurial firm depends on its capacity to learn. For such a firm, improvement is perpetually feasible, with inputs derived from all quarters: customers, employees, suppliers, staff, and management.

2. **The Production Chain: Consultive Coordination** Orthodox economic theory argues a market-plan dichotomy, wherein production phases are coordinated either via market pricing or hierarchical coordination. However, coordination within the new competition defies this dichotomy; "…*allowance must be made for consultive coordination or cooperation amongst mutually interdependent firms each of which specializes in distinct phases of the same production chain*" (1990:15). Technological shifts in one segment of the production chain may impact other segments. Such scenarios demand a specific problem solving capacity, best realized through long-term consultative network relationships rather than impersonal market exchanges or hierarchical control.

3. **The Sector: Competition and Cooperation** Beyond inter-firm coordination, a sector encompasses external facilities—such as trade associations, training programs, and joint marketing—that facilitate inter-firm activities. These facilities influence individual firms, their strategies, and their relative competitiveness vis-à-vis external sectors. In this perspective, firms engage in simultaneous competition and cooperation to generate joint services, establish the *rules of the market*, and execute complementary investments. Successful cooperation requires the formulation of clearly defined objectives and developing mechanisms to mitigate free-rider potential.

4. **The Government: Strategic Industrial Policy** The governmental role is inherently paradoxical: while cooperation helps long-term commitments to sectoral infrastructural development, competition ensures innovation and responsiveness to market opportunities. Drawing upon analyses of industrial policy in Japan and Italy, Best identifies three determinants of successful industrial policy. First is the creation and creative use of the market. Industrial policy falters when it disregards market forces, erroneously assuming market mechanisms and planning as mutually exclusive modes of coordination. The second element focus on a production focus over a distribution focus. A production orientation targets facilities that enhance production methodologies. Conversely, a distribution focus targets the allocation of production, often yielding deleterious

consequences; Wassenberg's (1988) compelling account of the restructuring of the Dutch shipbuilding industry is a case in point. The third element mandates that industrial policy be strategic, requiring goal formulation and identifying nascent sectors to maximize industrial growth.

§ 4.3.2 APPLICATION OF BEST TO CORE COMPETENCE MANAGEMENT

Based on his analysis, the organizational form Best advocates is the *industrial district*. *"Successful industrial districts are in a state of continuous restructuring as firms seek to remain competitive in a world of rapid technological change and intense international competition. For the competitive edge of firms in an industrial district comes from the combination of, first, high quality based on distinctive competences that result form specialization by phase within the production chain and, second, flexibility that results from the capacity for reconstruction of the micro production units along the production chain as technology advances and market conditions change. To capture these opportunities an industrial district must be collectively entrepreneurial"* (1990:234). Within these districts, the four previously articulated dimensions are critical. Regarding the dimension of 'the firm', the connection with core competence theory is manifest. The firm engages in a perpetual search for new opportunities and continuous improvement of products, processes, and methods to sustain competitive positioning, operating as a learning organization at every level.

Best, however, locates the source of competitiveness at the industrial sector level (*industrial district*). He notes that individual firms engage in vertical specialization within the production chain. While equating these vertical specializations with firm-level competencies requires a conceptual leap, accepting this premise highlights the criticality of consultative coordination. Alterations in a specific competence may impact others, particularly when the firm possesses internal problem solving capabilities. This necessitates a capability that fosters and protects information exchange, alignment, and development, enabling the firm to navigate and optimally exploit shifts. Consequently, this creates intra-firm network relationships that transcend SBUs, competencies, and hierarchical tiers.

Regarding the sector dimension, Best underscores the significance of facilitating activities occurring external to the firm yet impacting its operations. Through these activities, firms cooperate on shared services, market rules, and complementary investments. Critical to the efficacy of this facilitation is the precise articulation of cooperative objectives and the mitigation of free-rider problems. Applied to the corporate context, this dictates that a firm must not only explain its core competencies but also clarify their utility and strategic objectives. Moreover, Managerial Capabilities must establish the infrastructure necessary for network relationships to thrive. Concurrently, mechanisms must be devised to monitor and reward network participation and member effort, while discipline non-cooperation.

The government dimension further illuminates the facilitating function of Managerial Capabilities. Foremost is the institutionalization of the market within the firm. The market (Customer Value) must form the guiding strategic principle; strategy that ignores Customer Value is destined for failure. Additionally, a robust infrastructure facilitating the continuous improvement of core competencies needs to be established. The objective is not merely the allocation of resources across existing competencies, but the assessment of their improvement potential. Competencies must effectively compete for resources based on their improvement potential. Furthermore, Managerial Capabilities are tasked with identifying emerging competencies and prioritizing those demonstrating significant enhancement potential.

Best's concept of network relationships aligns well with holographic organizing principles. Managerial Capabilities are refined to a facilitative role, eschewing the imposition of rigid structures or methods, thereby enabling self-organization. This adheres to the principle of minimum critical specification. Learning to learn is exemplified by the firm's entrepreneurial orientation toward continuous product and process improvement. Furthermore, consultative coordination introduces redundancy, as various processes are rendered interdependent. A robust problem solving capability mandates the continuous sharing and exchange of knowledge to achieve integrated solutions. The requisite variety depends on environmental exposure, specifically regarding shifts in Customer Value and technological advancement. While Best does not explain the development or management of consultative coordination within networks—focusing instead on industrial policy—the concept of intra-firm networks (*core competence networks*) dedicated to knowledge exchange and the delivery of superior customer value is theoretically salient.

§ 4.3.3 PORTER: THE DIAMOND

In *The Competitive Advantage of Nations* (1990), Porter describes the determinants of national competitive advantage in specific industrial sectors. To this end, he proposes the *"national diamond,"* a framework comprising four interacting determinants: factor conditions, demand conditions, related and supporting industries, and firm strategy, structure, and rivalry. Factor conditions denote the nation's endowment of production inputs, including human capital, physical infrastructure, and natural resources. Demand conditions characterize the nature of domestic market demand, encompassing its scale, sophistication regarding price and quality, and its alignment with international demand patterns. Related and supporting industries refer to the presence of internationally competitive supplier clusters and related sectors. The final dimension, firm strategy, structure, and rivalry, encompasses the national context governing firm creation, organization, management, and the intensity of domestic competition. Furthermore, the external variables of government policy (e.g., regulation) and 'chance' events (e.g., natural disasters) influence both the determinants and their systemic interactions. These dimensions are interdependent; a favorable *diamond* confers upon firms the opportunity to establish and sustain competitive advantage relative to international rivals. Porter concludes that the immediate industrial cluster is pivotal for firm success, a centrality underscored by the related and supporting industries dimension. His principal thesis argues that robust domestic rivalry within the home country's *diamond* is the essential preparation for success in global competition.

§ 4.3.4 APPLICATION OF PORTER TO CORE COMPETENCE MANAGEMENT

A comprehensive summary of Porter's seminal work exceeds the scope of this analysis; consequently, the discussion is restricted to the strategic implications for firms and government (Chapters 11 and 12, respectively). From these chapters, pertinent elements are distilled and reviewed with respect to the components of core competence.

Knowledge Base The criticality of continuous product and process improvement, alongside knowledge expansion, is underscored by Porter's assertions: *"competitive advantage grows fundamentally out of improvement, innovation,* *and change; competitive advantage is sustained only through relentless improvement; and sustaining advantage demands that its sources be upgraded*" (1990:578; 580; 581). This perspective aligns fully with the frameworks of Prahalad & Hamel, Stalk et al., and Penrose.

Strategic mechanisms to achieve this include: "*source from the most advanced and international home-based suppliers, discover and highlight trends in factor costs, and maintain ongoing relationships with centres of research and the sources of the most talented people*" (1990:586; 588). Procuring from globally competitive suppliers allows firms to track state-of-the-art developments and technologies, while simultaneously challenging the firm to match external standards of excellence. Early detection of rising factor costs provides a temporal advantage, incentivizing efficiency gains or the substitution of inputs (1990:588). Furthermore, identifying and maintaining contact with key knowledge centers is paramount. Recruiting elite talent from reputable academic institutions injects the firm with novel ideas and capabilities.

Customer Value Porter similarly acknowledges the primacy of Customer Value, stating that "*competitive advantage involves the entire value system. Close and ongoing interchange with suppliers and channels is integral to the process of creating and sustaining advantage*" (1990:579). Active engagement with the value chain can be institutionalized through several ways. Firms should seek to serve the "*most sophisticated and demanding buyers and channels*" (1990:585). Such clientele function as a rigorous standard for performance and a source of critical feedback for product and process improvements. Similarly, serving customers with complex needs—those facing intense competition, high factor costs, or quality mandates—catalyzes internal improvement.

Additionally, identifying *lead users* allows firms to anticipate broader market trends (1990:588). Mandating that products "*significantly exceed all product standards*" (1990:585) stimulates innovation and contributes to the delivery of superior Customer Value. Anticipating regulatory or industry standards can yield competitive advantages and enhance brand reputation. Finally, the early analysis of emerging customer segments and distribution channels (1990:588) enables rapid response to nascent needs and preferences.

Managerial Capabilities In Porter's framework, Managerial Capabilities function as mechanisms to stimulate organizational innovation and improvement. This includes treating the workforce as permanent fixtures

(1990:586), which creates pressure to enhance productivity without expanding headcount, while potentially boosting employee motivation and engagement. Benchmarking against the dominant competitor is a further motivational catalyst (1990:586), focusing efforts on achieving superior differentiation and Customer Value. Furthermore, comprehensive competitive intelligence—covering both conventional and unconventional rivals—is essential to prevent strategic surprise (1990:588). Finally, integrating outsiders into the management team (1990:589) introduces cognitive diversity and fosters novel perspectives.

Managerial Capabilities assume a pivotal role in what Porter terms factor and demand conditions. Regarding factor conditions, education and training are paramount. *"Achieving more sophisticated competitive advantage and competing in advanced segments and new industries demands human resources with improving skills and abilities"* (Porter 1990:627–628). This encompasses not merely external education but also internal training designed to develop firm-specific capabilities and expand employee *repertoires*. Science and technology represent another critical factor condition (1990:630). This goes beyond the mere existence of an R&D department; it entails the scanning, assimilation, and mastery of relevant internal and external developments. Consequently, environmental openness and internal information exchange are prerequisites. Infrastructure forms a further factor condition (1990:637), with information and capital infrastructures being particularly salient. Information must be universally accessible, and capital must be allocated to its most effective locations. While seemingly evident, this is frequently neglected in practice. Information exchange is often inhibited by status anxieties, while capital allocation often follows historical inertia or responds to the most forceful demands. In the context of core competence management, capital allocation should ideally target organizational resources exhibiting the highest potential for competence growth.

Regarding demand conditions, the primary function of Managerial Capabilities lies in stimulating *"early and sophisticated demand"* (1990:651). This correlates with the aforementioned need that products and services exceed prevailing product and technological standards, ensuring the availability of sufficient intelligence regarding customers and, specifically, Customer Value (1990:652). Organizational structures must facilitate the implementation of novel ideas, requiring information access, technological proficiency, and self-organizing capabilities.

The preceding aspects align demonstrably with holographic organizing principles. Across all components, the necessity for sufficient knowledge, capabilities, information, and environmental openness is manifest. This creates redundancy precisely where it is requisite. Management must function in a stimulating and condition-generating capacity (*minimum critical specification*) to foster self-organization, thereby facilitating ideation and rapid adaptation. Furthermore, continuous improvement and innovation necessitate learning from error, a commitment to education and training to expand member *repertoires*, and the encouragement of organizational diversity. These elements form the core management tenets for building and expanding competencies to sustain competitiveness.

§ 4.4 CONCLUSION

To establish a conceptual framework for core competence management, this chapter has leveraged holographic organizing principles as formulated by Morgan (1986). This approach creates a perspective closely associated with facilitative management and self-organizing capabilities. While it may seem intuitive to manage core competencies through top-down directives—where the locus, methods, and timing of development are centrally determined—competence development is fundamentally rooted in creativity, problem solving, learning, capability deployment, and tacit experience. These factors are more effectively realized through a bottom-up approach, wherein management focuses on provisioning the necessary facilities and conditions, rather than through a *dirigiste*, top-down style.

This conclusion is corroborated by the theories of Best and Porter regarding sectoral and national competitive development, specifically regarding the upgrading of resources, capabilities, and competitive advantages. In these contexts, facilitative management also emerges as a critical driver of development. The subsequent chapter will further assert relationships between critical variables through the lens of analytical tools (management tools.

122

CHAPTER 5: TRADITION REVISITED

This chapter explores the possibility of integration of traditional analysis models into the core competence paradigm. The analysis revisits the original objectives of these models and translates them into the vernacular of core competence. While this adaptation may appear somewhat contrived, I argue that, within the specific context of core competence, these adapted models yield greater insight than their original formulations. These modifications are not definitive or exclusive means of adjustment; rather, they should be viewed as an exploratory exercise. These concepts were selected because their introduction catalyzed paradigm shifts in analytical thought and because they continue to exert a profound influence on management theory.

The adaptation potential of these concepts varies, as do the functions of the resulting models. The *competence curve* explains the relationship between two critical variables: the Knowledge Base and Customer Value. The *competence portfolio* serves as an instrument for resource allocation. *Competence strategies* offer a framework for evaluating the improvement, expansion, and transfer of firm competencies. Finally, the *competence chain* provides a methodology for identifying a firm's existing competencies. This latter concept is particularly significant, as it operationalizes the analytical methodology proposed in § 3.4.5.

§ 5.1 FROM *EXPERIENCE CURVE* TO *COMPETENCE CURVE*

The utility of a model lies in its ability to simplify 'reality' by isolating crucial variables for comparative analysis and establishing differentiation capabilities. The subsequent sections will first examine the criticality of the selected variables and their inherent differentiating power, which provide the basis for insight. The function of these variables will then be mapped onto their potential roles within the core competence concept.

§ 5.1.1 THE *EXPERIENCE CURVE*

The *learning curve* or *experience curve* plots cumulative production units against unit production costs. Empirically, as cumulative production volume increases, unit costs decline. This cost reduction is attributable partly to economies of scale—enabling more efficient capacity utilization or advantageous input procurement—and partly to the experience effects accrued through the production of a specific good.

In the mid-1960s, the *Boston Consulting Group* demonstrated that this experience effect extends beyond production to encompass all value-added costs, including administration, sales, marketing, and distribution. They established that unit costs decrease by a relatively constant percentage (typically between 10 and 30%) with each doubling of cumulative output (Abell & Hammond 1988:563).

Figure 5.1

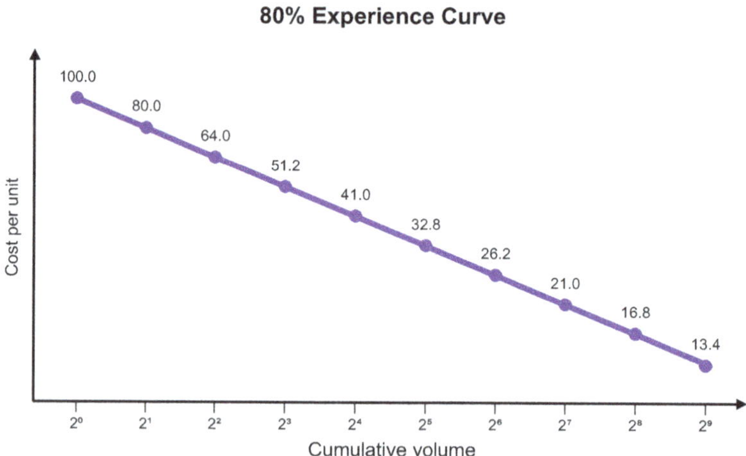

The experience curve can be expressed by the function $k(x) = a * x^b$, where $k(x)$ denotes marginal cost, a represents the cost of the first unit produced, x is the cumulative production quantity, and b is the experience elasticity. When plotted on a logarithmic scale, this relationship appears linear.

A salient implication of this concept is that firms should strive for maximum market share to augment sales volume and leverage cost-reduction opportunities, thereby securing competitive advantage. However, since this potential is accessible to all market participants, it needs to traverse the experience curve more rapidly than rivals. Achieving market leadership allows a firm to preempt competitors from attaining lower cost structures.

This concept is firmly situated within the *Financial Planning* phase, based on a stable competitive environment that supports long production runs, minimal design fluidity, and price-based competition. This limitation forms the basis of the primary critique: the model's applicability is restricted to price-competitive contexts, a condition that has been increasingly rare in the last decade. Furthermore, the prevalence of saturated markets and rapid technological change diminishes the concept's contemporary relevance.

"While there must be a theoretical limit to the amount by which costs can ultimately be reduced, a manufacturer reaches the practical limit first. However, the practical limit is not reached because he has exhausted his means of cutting costs; it is rather determined by the market's demand for product change, the rate of technological innovation in the industry, and competitors' ability to use product performance as the basis for competing" (Abernathy & Wayne 1974:118). A further critique argues that the experience curve is not an automatic phenomenon; it demands substantial managerial intervention. Thus, experience does not cause reductions but rather provides an opportunity that alert managements can exploit (Abell & Hammond 1988:566).

§ 5.1.2 THE *COMPETENCE CURVE*

In the Schumpeterian environment described in Chapter 1, which characterizes the operational reality for a significant proportion of contemporary firms, the experience curve is no longer fully applicable. Technological change is accelerating, consumer sensitivity has shifted from price to performance, and product lifecycles have contracted. Nevertheless, the experience curve contains a fundamental premise that intuitively resonates with the core competence concept: experience is accrued through the repetitive execution of an activity, and this experiential potential is universally accessible.

From a core competence perspective, this study argues that the critical variable is not cumulative production volume, but rather the cumulative magnitude of Customer Value delivered. Customer Value is less susceptible to volatility arising from technological shifts, specific product iterations, or market fluctuations. Being more abstract, it possesses greater stability. Furthermore, the dependent variable need not be cost, particularly given the prevalence of product-led competition (Best 1990) where performance is paramount. As demonstrated in preceding chapters, a correlation exists between the volume of Customer Value delivered and the firm's Knowledge Base; the delivery of Customer Value generates potential for knowledge expansion. I propose that in the context of the core competence concept, this relationship—Customer Value vis-à-vis Knowledge Base—as the primary focus, replacing the traditional volume-cost dynamic.

Figure 5.2

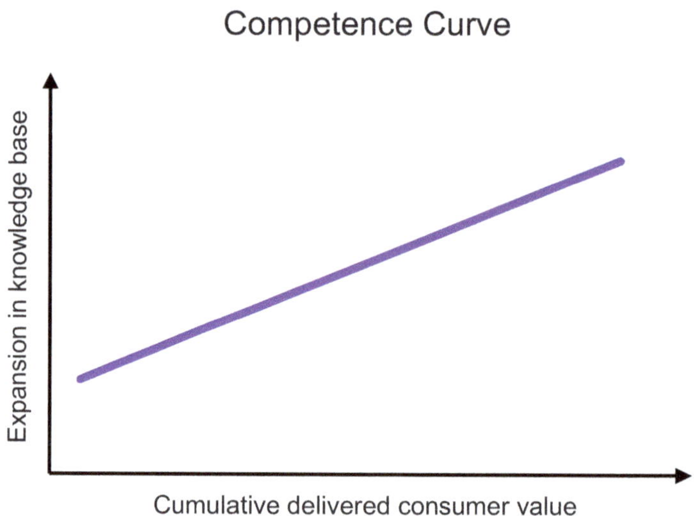

The competence curve is depicted here as linear to illustrate a positive correlation between the Knowledge Base and Customer Value. However, it is plausible that this relationship may manifest as a progressive, degressive, or S-curve function (contingent upon firm typology and the specific selection-environment). This variance warrants further empirical investigation.

This framework addresses the aforementioned criticisms in several ways. As previously articulated, Customer Value forms a more stable analytical baseline than aggregate unit output. Customer Value is not tethered to a singular product variant but rather transcends multiple iterations. Furthermore, demand for a specific category of Customer Value exhibits greater stability than demand for a specific product. Consequently, the previously identified 'practical limit' of cost reduction is circumvented. By correlating this with the Knowledge Base, the model also accommodates the model-based shift from price-led to product-led competition, wherein the focal point is product performance.

In product-led competition, price assumes a subsidiary role. The development of products that satisfy customer requirements necessitates the expansion of the Knowledge Base; this need is delineated in the competence curve. Viewed through the lens of core competence components, this process is demonstrably non-automatic. Managerial Capabilities are pivotal in facilitating both the delivery of Customer Value and the development of the Knowledge Base, as well as in ensuring the strategic alignment of these two components.

Whether this concept can be quantified as readily as the original model remains a pertinent question. While the cumulative magnitude of delivered Customer Value is quantifiable, the measurement of the Knowledge Base presents significant methodological challenges. While specific competencies permit quantification—such as technological competencies via patent metrics or sales competencies via customer volume—this approach is overly simple. Competencies, particularly those defined functionally, cannot and should not be analyzed in isolation. A core competence transcends the parameters of a singular technological competence. Consequently, it may be more rigorous to employ this concept as a qualitative instrument, assessing the Knowledge Base primarily in qualitative terms. This approach facilitates both internal comparative analysis of distinct core competencies and external benchmarking against competitors.

§ 5.2 FROM *PRODUCT PORTFOLIO* TO *COMPETENCE PORTFOLIO*

§ 5.2.1 THE *PRODUCT PORTFOLIO*

In the 1960s, many firms operated under the assumption that effective management did not depend on detailed business-specific knowledge, but rather on the application of universalistic management paradigms. This perspective was viable partially due to the prevalence of high-growth markets, which obscured strategic errors, and, consequently, highly diversified conglomerates proliferated.

This diversification rendered firm management increasingly complex and opaque. A distinct need arose for a methodology to map the firm's diverse activities, thereby facilitating decision-making—specifically regarding the identification of cash-generating units versus those requiring investment based on favorable market prospects. The *Boston Consulting Group* addressed this requirement with the *growth/share matrix*. Subsequently, every prominent consultancy developed a proprietary variation of this method. Notable examples include the *General Electric–McKinsey* industry *attractiveness/business position matrix*, *Arthur D. Little's* industry *maturity/competitive position model*, and the *Shell Directional Policy matrix* (Haspelagh 1982:61). This analysis restricts itself to the original concept developed by the *Boston Consulting Group*.

The *growth/share matrix* plots market growth against the relative market share of a product, activity, or Strategic Business Unit (SBU). Within the matrix, a product/SBU's position is represented by a bubble, the diameter of which corresponds to market size. This facilitates the mapping of diverse products/SBUs based on two critical variables. Market growth theoretically corresponds to the product life cycle. A product's market position is assessed via its competitive standing: relative market share. This market share, in turn, correlates with the experience curve discussed in the preceding section.

The matrix is quadrant-divided into four domains: *cash cow*, *dog*, *question mark*, and *star*. The underlying logic dictates that the cash flow generated by the *cash cow* be deployed to fund *question marks*, financing the substantial investment required to capture market share and evolve into a *star*. A *star* should be self-financing, while a *dog* warrants no investment and is a candidate for divestiture. Thus, the *growth/share matrix* functions primarily as a mechanism for resource allocation (Henderson 1979:165).

Figure 5.3

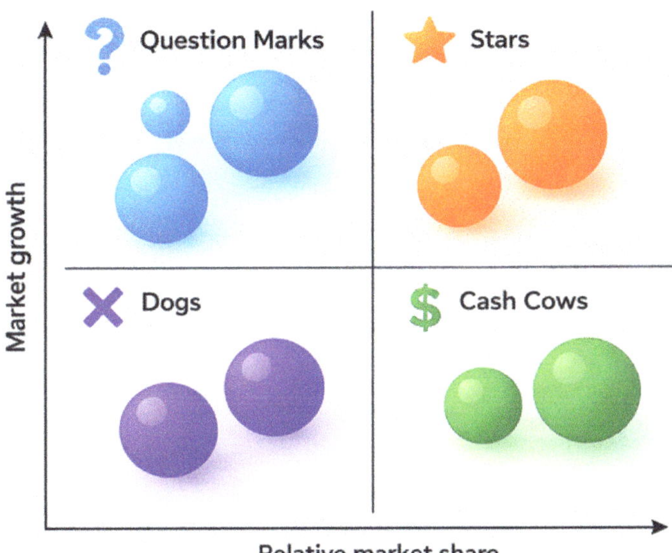

Classifying products/SBUs according to their operational market and competitive position is intuitively logical. Furthermore, the graphical representation is lucid and accessible. However, the method purports a level of objectivity that it does not entirely uphold. A central methodological deficiency concerns the definition of the market. A broad definition risks obscuring the growth profiles of specific market segments, whereas a narrow segmental analysis may neglect broader market dynamics. This definition also dictates the composition of the competitor set used to determine relative market share; competitors may be arbitrarily excluded depending on the market scope. Further objectivity issues arise in establishing the market growth rate: should this rely on historical data, near-term projections, or long-range forecasts? Consequently, the method lacks the objectivity it seemingly projects. Additionally, it is arguably reductionist. Allocating resources based exclusively on these two variables can precipitate significant strategic errors.

From the vantage of core competence theory, the divestiture of a dog is not invariably prudent, as it may contribute critically to a core competence. The fundamental flaw is the analysis's myopic focus on the product to the exclusion of value—both value to the firm and value to the customer. Furthermore, a *cash cow* offers utility beyond mere extraction ('milking'); it can serve as a launchpad for high-potential activities. *"A cow can give more than milk; properly exposed to outside influences and environmental forces, a cow can also give calves"* (Seeger 1988:604).

The preceding points summarize the primary critiques of the product portfolio. Several pragmatic limitations also exist, such as the ambiguity of a product situated in the liminal center of the matrix. Additionally, the product portfolio fails to indicate where new activities should be initiated. However, it must be recognized that the matrix is merely a practical tool for visualizing the firm's position. It cannot replace the executive function of management.

§ 5.2.2 THE *COMPETENCE PORTFOLIO*

Prahalad & Hamel (1990:86) previously argued that the product portfolio necessitates supplementation with a competence portfolio. Given the abbreviated lifecycles characterizing contemporary products and markets, the traditional product portfolio proves inadequate. Conversely, mapping core competencies yields a more stable conceptualization, rendering it a superior foundation for long-term strategic analysis.

While examining market growth and relative positioning can be effective for products, it is inapplicable to core competencies. First, a core competence transcends specific markets, precluding precise, unambiguous market definition. Second, direct competitors possessing identical core competencies are rare; competitors may manufacture identical products utilizing distinct core competencies. Consequently, determining relative market share regarding core competencies is methodologically fraught. I contend that two alternative variables are critical for mapping core competencies: the relative share of delivered functionality and the improvement potential of the core competence. This approach illuminates the positioning of core competencies, facilitating resource allocation based on improvement potential and the demand for specific functionalities.

As previously established, the functionality of a core competence forms a more stable variable. This metric can serve as a basis for competitive benchmarking, replacing relative market share. Consequently, the firm is compelled to analyze competitors regarding their share of functionality.

Crucially, a core competence pertains to underlying functionality rather than being tethered to a specific product. Revisiting the Xerox and Canon example (§ 1.4): Xerox may have defined its competence as document copying and viewing Canon's competence as image photography. Here, copying is linked to the photocopier and photography to the camera. Yet, both address an identical functionality—image reproduction—regardless of whether the source is physical media or the surrounding environment.

The second variable, improvement potential, assesses the firm's capacity to enhance its core competencies. This is paramount, as it forms the central objective of core competence management. Sustained competitiveness is contingent upon the continuous improvement of core competencies. Furthermore, as demonstrated in § 4.4, resource allocation is optimized when based on improvement potential (Best 1990:20).

Figure 5.4

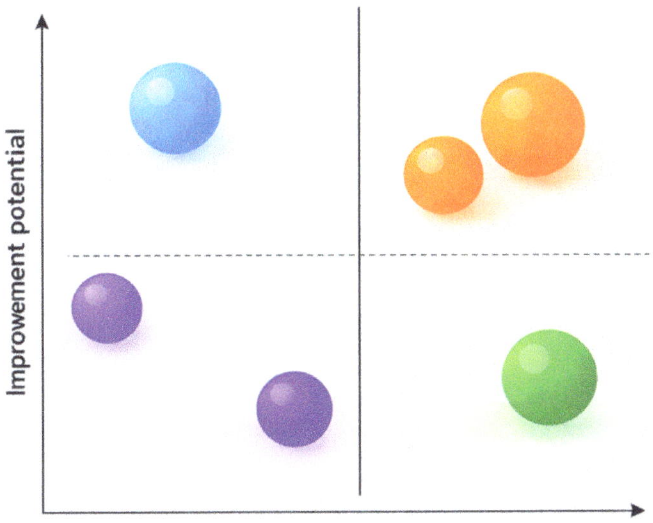

A salient attribute of this portfolio specification is that a core competence in a *dog* position (left bottom quadrant) does not automatically warrant divestiture. Conversely, it should stimulate relevant core competence networks (refer to § 4.3.2) to investigate improvement Xent opportunities, thereby benefiting the firm. The practical limitation of the product portfolio—its failure to indicate where to initiate new activity—is less relevant here. Core competence theory suggests that new activities logically emanate from existing ones (*path dependency*).

Comparing this portfolio with the product portfolio reveals similar challenges regarding objectivity. Issues arise concerning the definition of functionality, the temporal horizon, and the scope of competitive analysis. However, it must be argued that this model serves merely as a practical instrument for differentiation; management retains the need to interpret the aggregate data rather than applying the model mechanically.

This approach prioritizes the value of the core competence—value derived by both the firm and the customer. Consequently, products that are critical from a core competence perspective, yet occupy a *dog* status, cannot be summarily discarded, as they contribute to improvement potential and demand generation. As previously noted, this portfolio aligns with the managerial assessment required for resource allocation, which may be executed in a manner analogous to the original concept.

§ 5.3 FROM *DIVERSIFICATION STRATEGIES* TO *COMPETENCE STRATEGIES*

§ 5.3.1 *DIVERSIFICATION STRATEGIES*

Ansoff (1987:109) pioneered the observation that firms possess distinct growth opportunities through diversification. He developed the *growth vector*, which generates four growth domains based on product (existing/new) and market (existing/new) variables. *Market penetration* denotes existing products in existing markets, where the firm seeks to augment share in served markets. *Product development* involves introducing new products to existing markets to increase share. *Market development* entails deploying existing products in new markets to expand revenue. Finally, *diversification* involves operating in new markets with new products. Based on this growth vector, a firm determines the trajectory of its *strategic portfolio*.

Figure 5.5

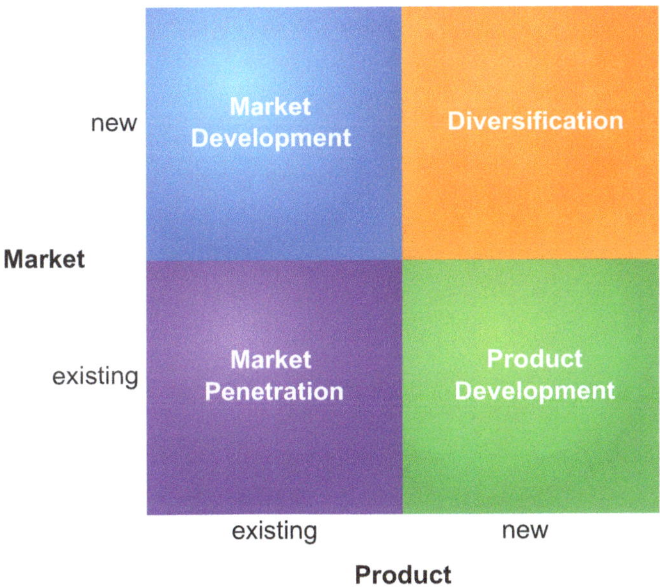

Diversification is manifestly the most perilous strategy, given the firm's limited knowledge of both product and market. This is corroborated by Rumelt (1982:363), who demonstrated that related constrained diversification yields the highest profitability, whereas unrelated diversification correlates with the poorest performance. Nonetheless, this growth vector was frequently selected in the 1960s, driven by the prevalence of growth markets and the erroneous belief in the fungibility of management expertise across disparate activities. A further deficiency is the absence of prescriptive rules for selecting diversification targets.

§ 5.3.2 *COMPETENCE STRATEGIES*

As indicated, the variables of 'product' and 'market' are becoming increasingly difficult to apply. From the perspective of the core competence concept, a critical deficiency is that the relationship between these product–market combinations and core competencies is undefined. I therefore propose synthesizing the relationship between core competencies and these product–market combinations.

These product–market combinations may be categorized as *core* and *non-core business*. Similarly, the variable of competence may be subdivided into *core* and *non-core competence*. This framework outlines four distinct strategies for competence growth, explained here via a model-based example. Consider a firm such as McDonald's, where the core competence can be defined as 'providing customers, in the shortest possible time, with a certain type of food (snack) that has consistent quality'. Investments directed toward existing competencies within the core business result in competence improvement. For instance, capital allocation aimed at accelerating the delivery speed of the existing product portfolio fosters the enhancement of this established competence.

Figure 5.6

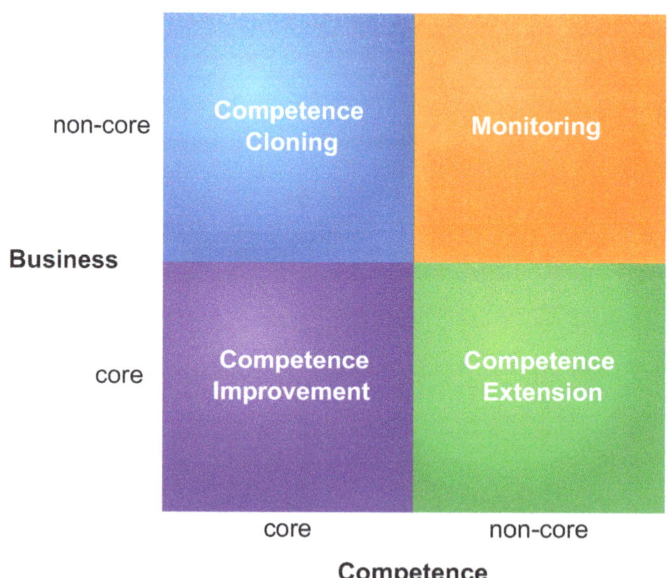

Conversely, investments in non-core competence within the core business facilitate the potential expansion of the competence. In this context, one might consider investments in on-site childcare amenities. Such additions augment the dining experience for both parents and children, thereby expanding the competence to encompass a dimension of experiential value or 'dining enjoyment'.

Investments dedicated to transferring existing competencies to a non-core business form the replication of the competence. This might manifest as the rapid service of high-quality haute cuisine. In this scenario, the existing operational competence is effectively transposed or 'cloned' into a non-core business domain.

The fourth quadrant involves investments in a non-core business utilizing non-core competence. The strategic function of such investments is primarily exploratory—scanning and monitoring activities that may evolve into future competencies or address nascent functional demands. For example, the firm might invest in sustainable food preparation, eco-friendly packaging, and waste segregation. It is conceivable that such services could eventually be commercialized to other restaurants, thereby fostering a core competence in the environmental domain. However, the limitations inherent in Ansoff's original model persist here. The identification of optimal diversification targets (or monitoring subjects) remains problematic, and Managerial Capabilities often lack fungibility across disparate markets and product categories.

§ 5.4 FROM *VALUE CHAIN* TO *COMPETENCE CHAIN*

§ 5.4.1 THE *VALUE CHAIN*

In *Competitive Advantage* (1985), Porter introduced the value chain construct. He argues that competitive advantage is inexplicable when viewing the firm as a monolithic entity. Rather, competitive capability *"…stems from the many discrete activities a firm performs in designing, producing, marketing, delivering, and supporting its product. Each of these activities can contribute to a firm's relative cost position and create a basis for differentiation"* (Porter 1985:33). The firm's *value chain* is embedded within a broader value system, which encompasses supplier value chains, channel value chains, and buyer value chains.

Porter establishes the SBU as the unit of analysis: *"The relevant level for constructing a value chain is a firm's activities in a particular industry (the business unit)"* (Porter 1985:36). The value chain outlines total value, defined as the price buyers are willing to pay. It comprises value activities and the margin, which together form total value. Value activities are bifurcated into primary and support activities. Primary activities *"…are the activities involved in the physical creation of the product and its sale and transfer to the buyer as well as after-sale assistance"*, whereas support activities *"…support the primary activities and each other…"* (Porter 1985:38).

Porter categorizes primary activities as follows: inbound logistics (receiving, warehousing, and input distribution); operations (transformation of inputs into final products); outbound logistics (collection, storage, and distribution to customers); marketing and sales (facilitating purchase and persuasion); and service (maintenance or enhancement of product value). Support activities are defined as: procurement (the function of purchasing inputs, distinct from the inputs themselves); technology development (product and process improvement); human resource management (recruitment, hiring, training, and development); and firm infrastructure (activities supporting the entire value chain rather than individual components, such as general management, planning, and legal counsel).

Within each activity category—both primary and support—three distinct types are discernible: *direct* activities (creating direct buyer value), *indirect* activities (sustaining ongoing operations), and *quality assurance* activities (determining output quality). While indirect and quality assurance activities are frequently undervalued in analysis, they are critical determinants of cost structure and differentiation.

The value chain is dynamic rather than static. The identification of relevant value activities is contingent upon specific criteria: their impact on differentiation potential and their proportion of total cost. Consequently, these vary across firms. Activities must be categorized to optimally reflect their contribution to competitive advantage. For instance, while order processing is typically classified under outbound logistics, for a distributor, it may represent a critical component of marketing. Furthermore, the linkages between value activities are paramount. *"Although value activities are the building blocks of competitive advantage, the value chain is not a collection of independent activities but a system of interdependent activities"* (Porter 1985:48). Interdependencies influence the execution and cost of related activities. Competitive advantage may thus be derived through optimization and coordination. Optimization generally entails managing trade-offs between distinct activities achieving the same outcome. Coordination, beyond yielding cost reductions, can also generate differentiation opportunities.

Figure 5.7

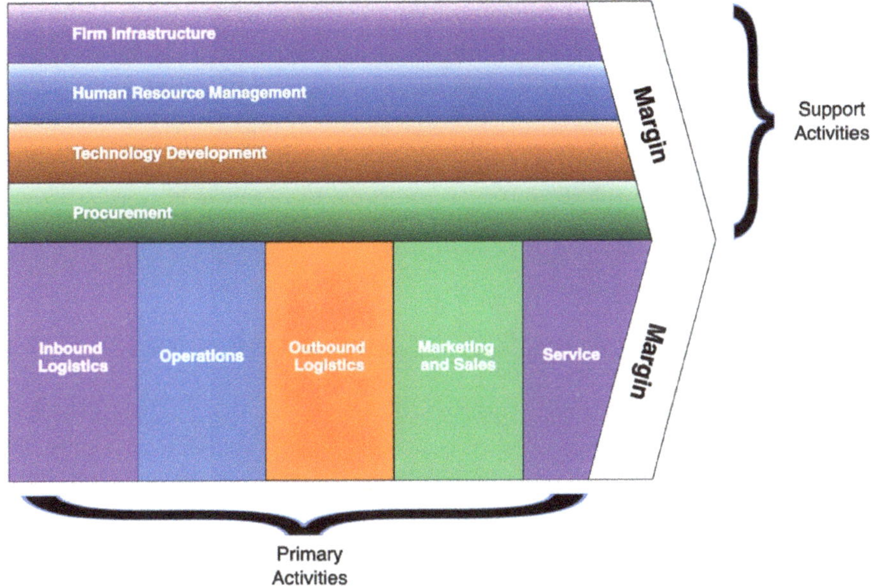

Source: Porter (1985), p.37

While the value chain offers a robust methodology for mapping value-creating activities, it presents a limitation when viewed through the lens of core competence theory: the SBU level of analysis. Consequently, critical value-creating activities may be obscured. These essential activities frequently transcend SBU boundaries and are thus excluded from standard analysis. The subsequent section explores methodologies to resolve this analytical discrepancy.

§ 5.4.2 THE *COMPETENCE CHAIN*

Because core competencies typically transcend SBU boundaries, a unitary value or competence chain is required to represent the firm's aggregate core competencies. The *Boston Consulting Group* (BCG) differentiates between *core capabilities* and *core competencies*. They conceptualize core competencies primarily as domain knowledge—the technical and economic expertise requisite for a specific business, including know-how regarding production techniques, material handling, and quality assurance (interview with M. Raida, Boston Consulting Group Düsseldorf). Conversely, capabilities are viewed as cross-functional processes spanning diverse business units, such as time-based competition, logistics, information flows, and environmental management. This distinction underpins what BCG terms a *"Strategic Platform"* (Boston Consulting Group 1992:17), previously alluded to in Chapter 1 as the *grand unifying theory*.

Figure 5.8

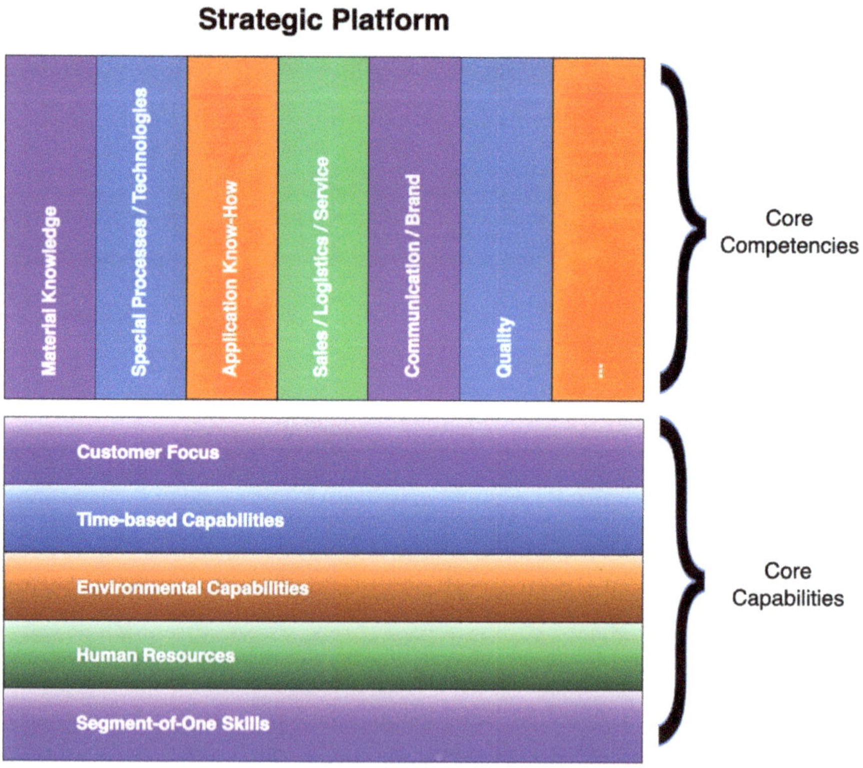

Boston Consulting Group 1992:17

"We are convinced that competitive success can no longer be defended solely through a firm's position within its business domain (as expressed in market share and economies of scale), but increasingly through core competencies and cross-business capabilities (e.g., speed, information advantages, and levels of training)."

"Accordingly, organizational performance can no longer be determined solely by the sum of its individual parts (profit-center thinking), but rather, and critically, by the behavior of the system as a whole" (Boston Consulting Group 1992:17).

This strategic platform may be reconceptualized as a corporate value chain. Herein, primary competencies are represented as core competencies (per BCG's taxonomy), while supporting competencies appear as capabilities. Mapping this to the framework established in Chapter 3, core competencies align broadly with the Knowledge Base, while core capabilities correspond to Managerial Capabilities. Inclusion of specific competencies is contingent upon their contribution to Customer Value creation. Consequently, the inter-activity relationships identified by Porter assume critical significance. As demonstrated in Chapter 3, the interaction between core competence components is pivotal for competence generation. This perspective explains the systemic interrelationships among diverse competencies.

A limitation of this *competence chain* is its construction at the corporate macro-level, which obscures the granular composition of individual core competencies. Furthermore, it lacks a mechanism for competence identification. Chapter 3 introduced an analytical methodology broadly outlining loci for competence identification. This can be operationalized by adapting Porter's original value chain. Porter analyzes value-creating activities; by assessing these activities specifically for their contribution to Customer Value, one gains insight into firm competencies. Porter's primary activities explain organizational routines, while support activities highlight critical Managerial Capabilities. Since the evaluation criterion is contribution to Customer Value, all three core competence components are integrated, facilitating a holistic perspective.

The analytical process is structured as follows: Initially, Porter's *value chain* is employed to identify all activities delivering Customer Value. Crucially, this analysis is conducted at the corporate level rather than the SBU level. Although resource-intensive, this macro-analysis is necessary to capture cross-SBU activities and reveal underlying structural commonalities masked by artificial SBU delineations. This process clarifies the attribution of activities to either the Knowledge Base or Managerial Capabilities. Subsequently, the interrelationships between activities are examined to reveal systemic interconnections, allowing for the assessment of the firm's competence maturity. It then becomes feasible to re-aggregate activities by core competence. Thus, a specific value chain—or more accurately, a *competence chain*—can be constructed for each core competence. In this model, Knowledge Base activities function as primary activities, supported by Managerial Capabilities. Constructing a competence chain for each core competence (or competence stage) exposes gaps in Customer Value creation, missing linkages, and opportunities for improvement or expansion. At the corporate level, the strategic platform is then synthesized from these distinct *competence chains*, providing both a comprehensive overview of core competencies and a framework for strategic discourse regarding long-term direction.

§ 5.5 CONCLUSION

This chapter has demonstrated that established strategic concepts are not directly fungible within the core competence paradigm. Consequently, I have proposed modifications to these models, specifically altering the variables employed or the mode of their application.

This necessity arises because traditional variables—price, cost, and market share—lack centrality within core competence theory. Instead, variables such as Customer Value, Managerial Capabilities, the Knowledge Base, and the improvement potential of core competencies are paramount. Given that the original concepts possess analytical techniques for differentiation, I elected to retain the underlying methodologies while substituting the variables. While this adaptation may seem abstract, it successfully explains essential relationships between key variables, making the refined methodologies no less relevant than their predecessors.

CHAPTER 6: CONCLUSION

This chapter synthesizes the findings of the preceding analysis. To this end, the core competence theory developed herein is juxtaposed with existing core competence concepts to assess comparative validity. Furthermore, the practical applicability of the framework is examined through a case study detailing the core competence analysis process at De Koninklijke Nedlloyd Groep NV (Nedlloyd). The chapter concludes by addressing critiques of the core competence concept and identifying avenues for future research.

§ 6.1 THEORETICAL CONTRIBUTION VIS-À-VIS EXISTING LITERATURE

Chapter 1 introduced three seminal concepts representing the dynamic capability approach and the *Strategic Leadership* phase: *core competence* (Prahalad & Hamel 1990), *resource-based analysis* (Collis 1991), and *core capability* (Stalk et al. 1992). This section provides a comparative analysis of the core competence and core capability frameworks against the model developed in this thesis. Comparison to the resource-based analysis is reserved for the subsequent section, where it will be discussed in conjunction with Collis's case study to bridge theory and practice. Regarding the core competence and core capability frameworks, this study argues that the concept advanced here offers superior generalizability, comprehensiveness, concreteness, and substantiation, thereby yielding deeper insight into the subject matter.

§ 6.1.1 COMPARATIVE ASSESSMENT: CORE COMPETENCE

Prahalad & Hamel (1990:82) analogize the firm to a tree: end products form the leaves, flowers, and fruit; SBUs represent the twigs; core products form the trunk and major branches, and core competencies are the roots. This metaphor is practically valuable, outlining distinct competitive dynamics at each level.

A comparison reveals that Prahalad & Hamel focus predominantly on the Knowledge Base and Customer Value. Crucially, they anchor the Knowledge Base primarily in technological proficiency; *"Core competencies are… especially how to coordinate diverse production skills and integrate multiple streams of technologies"* (Prahalad & Hamel 1990:82). While they do not reduce core competencies exclusively to technological capabilities, they regard these as the most significant and prevalent forms. Furthermore, they link Customer Value to the core product, defining core products as *"the components or subassemblies that actually contribute to the value of the end products"* (Prahalad & Hamel 1990:85).

From the perspective of this author's expanded core competence concept, this definition is restrictive. The Knowledge Base transcends technological know-how; it encompasses market intelligence, customer insight, and the capability to respond to shifting needs. Domains such as logistics and quality are frequently defined not by technology, but by service delivery capabilities, human resource management, and process optimization. Similarly, linking Customer Value exclusively to core products is reductionist. Customer Value denotes the differentiating quality or value perceived by the customer, relating to the holistic product or service rather than isolated components. The value proposition of a high-performance Honda engine is effectively neutralized if integrated into a Lada chassis. Such a hybrid would fail to replicate Honda's commercial success, as value is multidimensional—encompassing aesthetics, comfort, quality, and service. For instance, Honda's dealer management is distinguished by *"…its ability to train and support its dealer network with operating procedures and policies for merchandising, selling, floor planning, and service management"* (Stalk et al. 1992:66). Consequently, Customer Value must be associated with the totality of the product-service offering.

Prahalad & Hamel accord insufficient attention to the Managerial Capabilities requisite for realizing core competencies. While they identify the objective—to *"…create an organization capable of infusing products with irresistible functionality or, better yet, creating products that customers need but have not yet even imagined"* (Prahalad & Hamel 1990:80)—they do not identify the functional mechanisms to accomplish this. They advocate for clear strategic intent and centralization yet paradoxically assert that *"[t]he real sources of advantage are to be found in management's capability to consolidate corporatewide technologies and production skills into competencies that empower individual businesses to adapt quickly to changing opportunities*" (Prahalad & Hamel 1990:81). This tension suggests a need for facilitative management and self-organizing capabilities at the decentralized level, as detailed in Chapter 4. Rigid centralization inhibits rapid adaptive response—the very deficiency that precipitated the SBU paradigm (Dongen van 1993:7). Re-centralization offers no panacea; however, efficacy may be restored if centralization is restricted to facilitative functions. This logic aligns with Prahalad & Hamel's observation that SBUs should compete not only for capital but also for competence carriers (1990:91).

The systemic interactions between Managerial Capabilities, Knowledge Base, and Customer Value remain under-theorized in their work. Chapter 3 demonstrated that these interactions—including the explication of mental models, double-loop learning, and the institutionalization of Customer Value in organizational routines—are critical for competence development and maintenance. The Van Gelder case (§ 3.2.4) further illustrates the importance of these interactions.

Finally, Prahalad & Hamel fail to proffer a methodological framework for competence identification. Section 3.4 addresses this gap by providing a general analytical approach based on end products, firm processes, SBU/corporate infrastructure, and benchmarking.

While the framework presented in this study requires further concretization, it establishes a conceptual basis for competence audit. Prahalad & Hamel allude to the necessity of a strategic architecture, diversification implications, and a competence portfolio, yet leave these concepts largely undeveloped. Chapter 4 operationalizes strategic architecture via four holographic organizing principles: redundancy of functions, minimum critical specification, learning to learn, and requisite variety (elaborated in further detail in Appendix C). Chapter 5 provides an examination of associated strategic concepts, including competence strategies and the competence portfolio.

In summation, the core competence concept advanced herein is demonstrably more comprehensive and theoretically substantiated than the model presented by Prahalad & Hamel. However, acknowledgment is due to their pioneering elaboration of the concept, which provided the foundational bedrock upon which this analysis is built.

§ 6.1.2 COMPARATIVE ASSESSMENT: CORE CAPABILITIES

Stalk et al. (1992) approach the core competence construct from the vantage point of firm processes. A process is deemed strategic when it commences and concludes with the customer. Consequently, the operational focus is the delivery of Customer Value. Stalk outlines four foundational assumptions: 1) strategic processes form the fundamental building blocks of corporate strategy; 2) competitive success is contingent upon the transformation of key functional processes into strategic capabilities; 3) strategic infrastructure investments are required to bridge and transcend traditional SBU silos; and 4) strategic stewardship resides with executive management (Stalk et al. 1992:62). Adherence to these principles enables a firm to outperform rivals across five dimensions: 1) Speed: the rapid integration of shifting customer needs into new products; 2) Consistency: reliability in the delivery of Customer Value; 3) Acuity: the capacity to accurately diagnose the competitive environment and anticipate need shifts; 4) Agility: the flexibility to adapt simultaneously to divergent environments; and 5) Innovation: the generation of novel ideas or value sources through the recombination of existing elements.

The core capability model places primary emphasis on Customer Value and, secondarily, on Managerial Capabilities. *"Of course, just about every company these days claims to be 'close to the customer'. But there is a qualitative difference in the customer focus of capability-driven competitors. These companies conceive of the organization as a giant feedback loop that begins with identifying the needs of the customer and ends with satisfying them"* (Stalk et al. 1992:62). Regarding Managerial Capabilities, Stalk et al. advocate for identifying key processes, transforming them into strategic capabilities, synthesizing them into complex, inimitable chains, and capitalizing the requisite infrastructure. However, the specific operational mechanisms—the 'how'—remain underspecified.

The core competence concept advanced in this study aligns with Stalk regarding the primacy of Customer Value and the necessity of robust infrastructure. However, the integration of holographic organizational theory (Chapter 4) extends the analysis beyond Stalk et al.'s propositions. First, it explains the function of holographic organizing principles within the core competence framework and their managerial implications. Second, it clarifies the role of management in conditioning the environment for core competence development. While Stalk et al., like Prahalad & Hamel, position core competence management as a centralized need, they paradoxically note that *"…attribute of capabilities is that they are collective and cross-functional - a small part of many people's jobs, not a large part of a few"* (Stalk et al. 1992:63). This observation supports the argument for facilitative management and the promotion of self-organizing capabilities at the decentralized level.

Viewed through the lens of the core competence concept as advanced by this author, Stalk et al. accord insufficient attention to the Knowledge Base. While their 'strategic processes' partially correspond to organizational routines, they neglect the internal dynamics—specifically single-loop and double-loop learning and the emergence of path dependencies. The absence of a discourse on learning processes implies that process transformation is a discrete event rather than a continuous evolution. Conversely, they assert that complex strategic processes create barriers to imitation. *"The longer and more complex the string of business processes, the harder it is to transform them into a capability - but the greater the value of that capability once built because competitors have more difficulty imitating it"* (Stalk et al. 1992:62). This implicitly concedes the existence of learning processes and the necessity for competitors to replicate this learning curve, resulting in path dependencies (Collis 1991:50). Understanding these dynamics is critical for aligning Customer Value with the requisite infrastructure. The interactions between core competence components are decisive. The General Motors case (§ 3.2.4) serves as a potent illustration: a deficient Knowledge Base prevented GM from responding to shifting consumer requirements regarding fuel efficiency, safety, and environmental standards, causing a loss of market share to Japanese competitors.

The conclusion mirrors that of the previous comparison: the core competence concept presented here is more exhaustive and theoretically rigorous, offering deeper insight into the required internal processes of competence formation and management.

§ 6.2 EMPIRICAL RELEVANCE AND PRACTICAL APPLICATION

This section explores the practical utility of the core competence concept. The analysis leverages Collis's (1991) resource-based analysis of the ball bearing industry and a comparative review of the core competence analysis process at Nedlloyd.

It is argued that the core competence concept presented here offers a distinct perspective and superior insight compared to Collis's resource-based analysis, particularly regarding Customer Value. Furthermore, the core competence concept exhibits methodological parallels with the approach adopted by Nedlloyd.

§ 6.2.1 COMPARATIVE ASSESSMENT: RESOURCE-BASED ANALYSIS

Based on a review of the literature, Collis (1991:51) synthesizes two hypotheses regarding global competition that diverge from standard economic explanations. The first hypothesis argues that a firm's historical evolution "*…constrains its strategic choice and so will affect market outcomes.*" The second hypothesis suggests that "*...complex social phenomena…can be a source of sustainable competitive advantage and will affect organization structure independently of strategic choice.*" To operationalize these hypotheses, Collis identifies three elements of the resource-based view: *core competence, organizational capability*, and *administrative heritage.*

Collis defines core competence as "*…the vector of the irreversible assets along which the firm is uniquely advantaged*" (1991:51). He conceptualizes this vector as multidimensional, noting that prevailing descriptions often overly simply focus on a single dimension, such as technology or learning. A fundamental prerequisite is distinctiveness; only a unique or superior competence confers competitive advantage, necessitating rigorous competitive benchmarking. Organizational capability denotes "*…the managerial capability to continually improve and upgrade firm efficiency and effectiveness…*" (1991:52). Successful firms exhibit a collective capacity for innovation and environmental adaptation, facilitating continuous improvement. Administrative heritage encapsulates the organizational constraints governing strategic choice, comprising "*…both the intangible cultural heritage and the physical heritage of the firm*" (1991:52).

Leveraging these three elements, Collis formulates hypotheses to explain inter-firm differences. These hypotheses address why firms enter structurally unattractive markets, how national origin influences strategic choice, why organizational structure may diverge from strategy, and why administrative heritage can precipitate decisions that deviate from strict cost optimization.

Comparing resource-based analysis with the core competence concept advanced here reveals alignment: core competence aligns with the core competence definition (§ 3.2.4), organizational capability with Managerial Capabilities (§ 3.1.4), and administrative heritage with path dependency (§ 2.3.2). However, the conceptual treatment of their interrelationships differs. Collis's definition of core competence as a multidimensional vector remains abstract, lacking specification regarding the core dimensions and their systemic interactions. The core competence concept advanced here offers a substantially more granular explication of these dynamics.

Furthermore, this core competence concept integrates organizational capability (Managerial Capabilities) as a core element of core competence, rather than a discrete entity (§ 3.2). The systemic interactions between Managerial Capabilities and other competence components are critical for competence emergence and evolution. Consequently, organizational capability cannot be analyzed in isolation from the broader core competence construct.

From the perspective of the core competence framework, Collis's model notably neglects the dimension of Customer Value—a critical omission, as evidenced by the Philips case study (§ 3.2.4). A close reading of Collis's case study, however, reveals an implicit linkage between the core competencies of the three ball bearing manufacturers and the delivery of Customer Value, particularly regarding RHP and SKF. For instance, RHP's core competence is defined as "...*its technical engineering expertise... This allows it to respond quickly and effectively to a customer's request for a particular custom-designed bearing*" (1991:58). Similarly, SKF's competence is characterized as "...*its knowledge of, and capability to serve the needs of, its accumulated customer base with a complete range of bearings and products...*" (1991:58), underpinned by a philosophy of "*the right bearing in the right place*", facilitating "*the closest cooperation with [its] ever-expanding world network of customers, matching [its] bearing developments with technological breakthroughs in user industries*" (1991:58–59). While less explicit regarding Minebea, Collis locates its competence in "...*the process technology and production management skills needed for 'high-quality, volume production of precision products*" (1991:58). Minebea's strategy of low-cost via automation and high-quality via rigorous control effectively delivers Customer Value through a high-quality/low-cost proposition. As demonstrated in Chapter 3, Customer Value is intrinsic to core competence. Although Collis's analysis substantiate this, his resource-based analysis fails to theoretically formalize or integrate this dimension.

Evaluating Collis's case study through the lens of the core competence concept is constrained by the selective nature of his data presentation, which is tailored to his specific goals. Nonetheless, several observations are warranted. As previously noted, Collis implicitly connects core competencies to Customer Value without explicit theoretical acknowledgement. A similar lack of depth characterizes his treatment of organizational capabilities. The attributes he enumerates for each firm represent an undifferentiated amalgam of Knowledge Base, Customer Value, Managerial Capabilities, and their interactions. For SKF, he cites 24-hour off-the-shelf delivery, collaborative client learning, CAD/CAM infrastructure, and integrated order/delivery systems as organizational capabilities. For Minebea, he highlights the visionary leadership of Mr. Takahashi, knowledge transfer mechanisms between factories, and training initiatives. Regarding RHP, Collis identifies investments in flexible production alongside a strategic focus on a niche customer base capable of capturing specific value. I contend that this analysis lacks structural rigor. These elements could be mapped with greater efficacy using the core competence concept, which would more clearly explain the strategic rationale underpinning decisions.

Significantly, Collis observes that at SKF, organizational capability "...*is an integral part of the core competence which requires the ability to continually upgrade services to meet increasing customer demands. The organization is designed to anticipate, respond to, and integrate with the increasingly demanding needs of each of its three broad customer groups...*" (1991:61). From the standpoint of the core competence advanced here, this integration is definitive. The existence of a core competence is based on the alignment of all three components: Knowledge Base, Customer Value, and Managerial Capabilities. This systemic alignment offers a plausible explanation for SKF's resilience against low-cost competition from Japan and Thailand, enabling the firm to maintain a stable market share over a thirty-year period despite intense competitive pressure (Collis 1991:54).

§ 6.2.2 COMPARATIVE ANALYSIS: NEDLLOYD'S AUDIT

Appendix D details the historical evolution and operational scope of Nedlloyd. Circa 1970, the firm's primary focus was liner shipping, though merger activity had introduced ancillary operations such as tourism, aviation, and stevedoring. Over time, employing an "outside-in" strategic approach, several peripheral activities—specifically energy, road transport, aviation, and specialized transport—were elevated to core status (Oosterwijk 1988, p.308). This strategic pivot was driven by the profitability and growth potential inherent in these markets.

Despite this diversification, Nedlloyd retained a strategic fixation on mass and bulk operations, notably within the Liner Division and road transport sectors. Management operated under the presumption that the firm possessed the requisite Knowledge Base and Managerial Capabilities to sustain profitability (Financieel Dagblad 31-01-1989:3; 06-09-1989:3). However, these sectors suffered from a deficit in Customer Value; the service offering was commoditized, indistinguishable from competitors, and frequently disadvantaged by a higher cost structure (Oosterwijk 1988, p.310).

Conversely, profitability was concentrated in specialized activities, including specialized transport, heavy transport, Neddrill, and VGL (Annual Reports 1987–1991). These operations are distinguished by a distinct customer orientation and the requirement for domain-specific knowledge (e.g., chemical logistics, heavy lift, offshore drilling). Structurally, these activities tend to be project-based, a configuration that appears to align well with Nedlloyd's existing Managerial Capabilities.

Nevertheless, during periods of economic contraction, sectors such as aviation (Financieel Dagblad 23-03-1988; 08-04-1988) and energy (Financieel Dagblad 23-11-1990; 15-01-1991) were divested. These divestitures were rationalized as a strategic retrenchment to 'core activities', although Neddrill was retained, albeit ostensibly designated for sale.

Nedlloyd's strategy was defined by a philosophy of *vertical integration*, aiming to control the entire logistics chain (Oosterwijk 1988, p.309). This approach was likely influenced by the integrated models of Federal Express and DHL. However, whereas those integrators focus on high-value, time-sensitive segments (documents, parcels), Nedlloyd attempted to replicate this model within the Liner Division for undifferentiated general cargo. This proved unviable due to the absence of intrinsic Customer Value. Theoretically, had Nedlloyd succeeded in generating Customer Value within this context, it would have established a formidable barrier to imitation.

These strategic ambiguities prompted Nedlloyd to formally investigate its core competencies (based on interviews with H.J. Kiwiet and M. Vossenaar). Following a division heads' meeting, a dedicated project group was formed. The initial methodology involved surveying division heads regarding their perception of divisional and corporate core competencies. Despite the provision of foundational literature (Prahalad & Hamel 1990), the responses revealed a pervasive conceptual confusion regarding the definition of a core competence. The elicited responses were subsequently taxonomized into four categories: core competence, knowledge/skills, activities, and support. Examples ranged from specific technological knowledge to operational activities and IT infrastructure. Beyond categorization, the interrelationships between these elements were mapped to synthesize a coherent picture of the firm's perceived competence base. It is pertinent to note that, in the absence of established analytical tools for core competence auditing, Nedlloyd was compelled to develop a proprietary framework.

Utilizing this framework, Nedlloyd's activities were matrixed according to the delivery of Customer Value, distinguishing between two primary variables: process execution and process control. This yielded a four-quadrant typology. This classification was advantageous as it differentiated based on the intrinsic nature of the activity rather than the traditional modal split (maritime vs. terrestrial), thereby cutting across SBU silos. The quadrants were characterized as: *process management/solution driven*, *project management/timely solution driven*, *network management/system driven*, and *A-B management/demand driven*. Figure 6.1 illustrates the classification of the various operating companies.

Within two quadrants, Nedlloyd demonstrated operational success and a consensus regarding the existence of core competencies. However, the remaining two quadrants—comprising the majority of corporate assets— exhibited significant deficiencies. To address this, 'skill groups' were mobilized. The methodology involved an initial identification of essential capabilities via broad stakeholder consultation, followed by the definition of these skills and the formation of three dedicated groups per quadrant. The mandate of these groups was to articulate the strategic criticality of these capabilities, assess current maturity levels across operating companies, define target proficiency levels, and facilitate inter-unit knowledge transfer. Benchmarking extended beyond internal operations to include external comparisons to companies such as KLM, NS, and PTT.

Figure 6.1

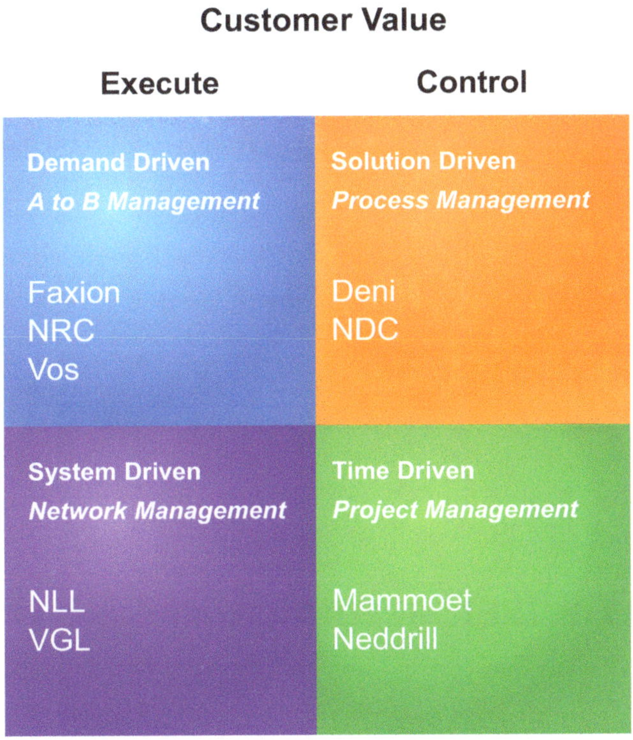

Customer Value

	Execute	**Control**
	Demand Driven *A to B Management*	**Solution Driven** *Process Management*
	Faxion NRC Vos	Deni NDC
	System Driven *Network Management*	**Time Driven** *Project Management*
	NLL VGL	Mammoet Neddrill

The outcomes were bifurcated: skill groups in one quadrant progressed effectively, whereas others encountered substantial obstacles. The primary impediment was the high degree of operational differences between firms among the core companies, which frustrated the establishment of a common lexicon and conceptual framework. Furthermore, inconsistent commitment from executive leadership caused momentum to dissipate. Consequently, the core competence management initiative has effectively stalled.

Comparing Nedlloyd's core competence analysis with the theoretical core competence concept advanced here reveals significant touch points. The taxonomy utilized—classifying elements into core competence, knowledge/skills, activities, and support—aligns substantially with the core competence components delineated in § 3.1. Specifically, 'knowledge/skills' maps to the Knowledge Base; 'support,' given the facilitative function of management, is analogous to Managerial Capabilities; and, as explained in § 3.4.1, the end products (here, activities) embody delivered Customer Value. The integration of these three components forms a core competence.

A methodological limitation nevertheless emerges from the data source, as reliance on division heads with unit-specific perspectives may obscure cross-divisional competencies. In contrast, an activity-based classification, which is inherently cross-divisional, helps to reduce this limitation. Categorizing activities according to Customer Value delivery is theoretically robust. A pertinent question concerns the generalizability of this classification: is it universal, or specific to Nedlloyd and the logistics sector? At best, this taxonomy is applicable to process-oriented service firms; it is likely ill-suited for product-manufacturing entities.

In summary, Nedlloyd's analytical process largely satisfied the criteria of the core competence framework. It is therefore lamentable that the initiative has stagnated. This outcome underscores the critical necessity of executive commitment and the need for top management to allocate sufficient resources to facilitate and sustain such strategic processes.

§ 6.3 CRITIQUES OF THE CORE COMPETENCE CONCEPT

The preceding analysis has focused on the necessity, mechanics, and organization of core competence management. Literature on core competencies and core capabilities frequently implies a degree of theoretical infallibility. This perspective is flawed; as Henzler (1988:1288) notes, emergent concepts should be viewed as corrective extensions of existing paradigms rather than wholesale replacements. The core competence concept must be evaluated through this lens, without neglecting its inherent limitations.

Leonard-Barton (1992:118) introduces the dialectic of *core rigidities* alongside core capabilities. Specialization in specific disciplines inevitably results in the underdevelopment of others, rendering the latter less attractive to organizational leadership. This creates friction in internal mobility (1992:119) and external recruitment; talent is less likely to join a firm where their discipline is peripheral (1992:118). Furthermore, physical systems may become sources of rigidity due to rapid obsolescence (1992:119). Crucially, "*[T]he very same values, norms and attitudes that support a core capability and thus enable development can also constrain it*" (Leonard-Barton 1992:119). These core rigidities represent the deleterious effects of path dependency. Managerial Capabilities must therefore encompass the capacity to manage and reorient these rigidities constructively.

Porter (1991:108) critiques core competence theory for its excessive internal focus, arguing that it neglects the external environment. While perhaps hyperbolic, this critique possesses merit. An exclusive focus on internal competencies risks strategic myopia. Monitoring and responding to environmental trends remain essential. Consequently, it is advisable to situate the core competence concept within a broader strategic framework. Philips serves as an illustrative case (sans normative judgment). Philips identifies four success factors (Dinklo 1992:2): 1) Vision: defining future activities and forecasting environmental evolution; 2) Strategy: comprehending the market, competitors, and positioning, while auditing strengths, weaknesses, and core competencies; 3) Team: recruiting, motivating, and empowering personnel; and 4) Action: translating objectives into operations with adaptive flexibility based on new insights. Regarding strategy and trajectory, the model distinguishes: 1) Vision ("seeing the unseeable"), which informs strategy; 2) Portfolio, entailing the selection of optimal product/market combinations; 3) Resources (human capital, finance, assets), which constrain opportunity exploitation; and 4) Capabilities, defined as accumulated knowledge and experience. The central proposition is that viable strategy cannot rely exclusively on capabilities. Capabilities must be embedded within a holistic framework, contingent upon available resources, existing product/market combinations, and strategic vision. This yields a more balanced strategy than one predicated solely on capabilities. While elements such as resources, team, and vision are implicit in the core competence concept (via path dependencies), their explicit inclusion serves to mitigate the risk of excessive internal focus.

A related observation is that path dependencies condition the availability of talent and financial capital. Consequently, firms face constraints in maintaining existing competencies and developing new ones. Given resource scarcity, firms must optimize allocation with a view toward future implications. Crucially, analysis must extend beyond competencies. Strategic timing, for instance, significantly influences the commercial success of products and their underlying competencies. For example, while Prahalad & Hamel (1990) attribute a core competence in optical media to Philips, the commercialization of the videodisc failed. While one might argue the core competence was immature, the timing was undeniably adverse given the concurrent rise of the videocassette recorder (Metze 1991:154). This demonstrates that products derived from core competencies do not guarantee market success, reinforcing the necessity of situating the core competence concept within a broader strategic context.

A significant risk emerges when core competence is conflated with specific technologies. While equating competence with technology is expedient due to its tangibility—a tendency prevalent in Prahalad & Hamel's work—this study argues such reductionism as a conceptual misapplication. Technology acts merely as a conduit for Customer Value, rather than constituting the value itself. Furthermore, tying competence to a specific technology exposes the firm to obsolescence via technological discontinuity and the longevity and validity of such competencies are contestable. Since the delivery of specific Customer Value often permits technological fungibility, a firm should ideally master a spectrum of technologies. Moreover, non-technological vectors—logistics, customer orientation, human capital, and quality—are equally critical. As Collis (1991:51) articulates, a core competence is inherently a "multidimensional vector."

§ 6.4 EVALUATION OF RESEARCH OBJECTIVES AND FUTURE DIRECTIONS

The subsequent sections assess the degree to which the research questions argued in the Introduction have been resolved. Following this evaluation, the analysis identifies critical lacunae remaining within the core competence paradigm.

§ 6.4.1 REVIEW OF OBJECTIVES

The primary objectives, as articulated in the Introduction, were:

- To explain the intellectual antecedents—specifically the foundational theories—of the core competence concept, thereby establishing a robust theoretical grounding.

- To synthesize these theories into a rigorous definition and functional description of core competence. The aim was to operationalize the concept beyond existing theoretical abstractions and to develop a methodological framework for competence identification.

- To delineate the organizational implications of core competence management. Given the paucity of literature addressing this domain, the objective was to construct a conceptual framework for the organization of competencies.

- To analyze the interface between core competence theory and established strategic concepts, assessing their compatibility and the potential for adaptation.

Chapter One contextualized the various core competence constructs within their temporal and model-based settings. Chapter Two excavated their intellectual roots, selecting theories (Schumpeter 1987; Penrose 1972; Nelson & Winter 1982) distinguished by an evolutionary perspective on the firm and industry—a stance aligned with the evolutionary nature of core competencies (§ 2.3.1, § 2.3.2). These theories span three distinct levels of analysis: Schumpeter offers a macro-economic perspective; Penrose provides a micro-level internal analysis; and Nelson & Winter bridge these with a meso-level analysis of the firm within a Schumpeterian environment. This multi-level theoretical triangulation facilitates a comprehensive treatment of the core competence spectrum.

These theoretical foundations enabled the formulation of a core competence definition, conceptualized less as a static lexical statement and more as a dynamic representation of component interactions (§ 3.2). These components are themselves derived from the foundational theories (§ 3.1). Thus, the objective of defining and elucidating the functioning of core competence has been realized. Regarding the concreteness of this conceptualization relative to existing literature, the comparative analysis in § 6.1 and § 6.2 suggests that the model developed herein is arguably more general, comprehensive, and operationally concrete. While further operationalization is always possible (and needed), the stated objective is deemed satisfied. Furthermore, developing a general analytical methodology addresses a significant gap in prior scholarship, which has largely neglected the mechanics of competence identification.

A central, yet underexplored, problematic concerns the organizational implications of core competence management—a topic virtually absent from the relevant literature. This study has developed a comprehensive organizational model that theoretically describes the processes conducive to competence enhancement. By applying the holographic organizing principles formulated in Chapter 3, this model achieves theoretical coherence, thereby more than adequately fulfilling the research objective.

Regarding the final objective—analyzing the interface between core competence theory and existing strategic concepts—the methodology involved a critical re-examination of established concepts through the lens of core competence. This required adapting the underlying logic of traditional strategic models to align with core competence assumptions. While inherently interpretive, the application of the theoretical framework minimized subjectivity. The resulting adapted concepts explain critical variable relationships within the core competence paradigm, sharpening the distinction from traditional strategic models. Supplemented by the contextual positioning in Chapter 1, this analysis successfully satisfies the stated objective.

§ 6.4.2 DIRECTIONS FOR FUTURE RESEARCH

Numerous inquiries remain unresolved. The most salient outstanding questions may be categorized as either theoretical or empirical. Two pivotal theoretical questions persist: first, what are the implications for the core competence construct when the unit of analysis extends beyond traditional firm boundaries? Second, is it feasible to isolate specific, measurable dimensions of a core competence?

The present analysis was restricted to the single firm, treating the firm boundary as a given. This study argues that intra-firm analysis sufficiently explains the primary mechanics of core competencies. However, complexity escalates significantly when the analytical scope encompasses joint ventures, strategic alliances, and similar inter-organizational arrangements. Such expansion amplifies both opportunities and risks, notably the potential for competence erosion. It is plausible that the internal relationships characterizing a core competence would require restructuring or reprioritization within these broader configurations.

The second critical question pertains to quantification. A defining attribute of core competencies is their uniqueness or superiority vis-à-vis competitors (Collis 1991:51). This necessitates determining the extent to which specific aspects of core competencies can be quantified to facilitate competitive benchmarking. While benchmarking is incorporated into the analysis methodology (§ 3.4), external comparative analysis presents significant methodological challenges. Identifying internal core competencies is inherently difficult; assessing external competitor competencies is exponentially more challenging. Consequently, this issue warrants rigorous investigation.

While a broad spectrum of empirical questions may be argued, the following are paramount. Longitudinal analyses of firms prioritizing core competencies are essential. The objective is to ascertain whether such firms achieve statistically superior performance metrics compared to those adhering to traditional paradigms. While existing literature is replete with case studies of successful competence-oriented firms, it is devoid of statistical corroboration. Although Stalk et al. (1992) offer a comparative analysis, a broader examination of this relationship across specific industries and strategic groups would be valuable.

Regarding the present study, empirical validation is highly desirable, particularly concerning the operationalization of the developed theory. Testing the framework within a live operational context would be advantageous. It is necessary to determine whether the formulated definition and analytical methodology yield actionable insights into firm-specific core competencies. Empirical testing would assess the theory's robustness and identify opportunities to enhance the model's concreteness and manageability. Similarly, the implementability of the organizing processes detailed in Chapter 4 requires verification. A practical case study would serve to validate the applicability and efficacy of these processes in satisfying the conditions for core competence management.

The concepts advanced in Chapter 5 also necessitate empirical verification. It is conceivable that certain variables may prove difficult to operationalize, while others may offer greater utility. Furthermore, these concepts may lack sufficient differentiating power or fail to adequately capture critical relationships. Empirical testing is thus requisite for conceptual refinement.

§ 6.4.3 CONCLUDING REMARKS

This concludes the study. I contend that this research has advanced the comprehension of the 'core competence' phenomenon. This contribution stems from a contextualization of the concept within both its temporal and model-based frameworks. Grounded in the resource-based paradigm, the core competence concept has evolved into the dynamic capabilities paradigm, which advocates for the continuous improvement and expansion of capabilities. Furthermore, the core competence concept addresses the heightened environmental turbulence that necessitates robust strategic leadership. The intellectual antecedents—specifically Schumpeter's *creative destruction* and *selection-environment*, Penrose's *productive services*, and Nelson & Winter's *organizational routines*—provide critical insight into the structural underpinnings of core competence. This synthesis establishes the theoretical depth and foundation of the core competence construct.

Moreover, the concept has been refined through a rigorous definition of core competence—the intersection of Knowledge Base, Customer Value, and Managerial Capabilities—, the delineation of competence stages, and developing a general analytical methodology. The analysis extends further, according significant attention to organizational implications—a domain largely neglected in prior literature. While articulating these consequences is complex, it is essential for practical application. Consequently, this study represents a substantive advancement in core competence theory and management.

Furthermore, the core competence concept has been juxtaposed with traditional theoretical frameworks. This critical comparison has yielded adapted or alternative conceptual applications compatible with the core competence paradigm.

Consequently, it is proposed that this research methodology be applied to future iterations of the core competence concept. Such analysis should scrutinize the positioning, theoretical foundations, definitional contributions, organizational implications, and inter-conceptual relationships of emerging variants

160

APPENDIX A

Philips (Based on Metze, 1991: "*Kortsluiting: hoe Philips zijn talenten verspilde*": 156–166)

In 1971, Philips pioneered the VCR system, debuting a device with a one-hour recording capacity at the Vidicom trade fair in Cannes. Competitors lagged by several years; Sony introduced the Betamax system in 1975, and Matsushita launched the VHS system in 1976. However, Philips committed a strategic error by agreeing to a market segmentation arrangement with Sony and Matsushita. Under this agreement, Philips restricted its operations to Europe for several years, while its competitors focused on Japan and the US. This interval provided Sony and Matsushita with a significant opportunity to penetrate the American market and refine their technology.

Philips subsequently replaced the initial N-1500 model with the N-1700, which featured a lower tape speed and extended recording duration. Crucially, the N-1700 lacked backward compatibility with N-1500 tapes, rendering existing media libraries obsolete—a decision detrimental to customer relations. Furthermore, the European market was less receptive to VCRs than the US market, and Philips' hardware suffered from quality control issues, resulting in frequent breakdowns. Retailers colloquially referred to the units as "carrier pigeons" due to their high rate of return for repairs. Consequently, when improved VHS and Betamax systems entered the European market in the late 1970s, Japanese manufacturers captured significant sales volume, aided by superior design.

Concurrently, Philips developed a third-generation VCR, the V-2000. This system distinguished itself from VHS and Betamax through two primary features: a reversible cassette allowing eight hours of recording (compared to three for Japanese competitors), which significantly reduced media costs, and microprocessor integration enabling channel storage and programmable recording up to sixteen days in advance. While technologically superior, the 1979 launch faced three immediate obstacles: competitor pricing had decreased significantly, the cost advantage of tape media had diminished, and the V-2000 suffered from reliability issues, with over 50% of units returned in 1980 due to head drum failures.

Operational limitations further hindered the system; programming was effectively restricted to four hours as remote tape reversal was impossible. Despite Philips' reputation for television image quality, the V-2000 offered no significant visual advantage over competitors. Furthermore, synchronization issues with Philips' own televisions occasionally resulted in superior performance when the VCR was paired with competitor displays (e.g., Sony). The V-2000's mechanical complexity, involving a higher component count, resulted in higher manufacturing costs. Although it achieved a 15% market share in Europe (and 30% in Germany) in its first year, VHS held 61% and Betamax 22%. Philips retained hope for market leadership given the projected growth of the European market, the primary theater of competition.

Philips' entry with a third format induced consumer caution, which also impacted sales of Japanese units as the market awaited a clear standard. Japanese manufacturers responded by initiating a price war. Philips subsequently alleged overproduction and dumping, as German mail-order retailers began selling Japanese recorders for under one thousand marks. Philips was compelled to match these reductions, lowering the V-2000's recommended price by 20% in November 1982. However, Sony remained 30% cheaper, with some alternatives costing half the price of a V-2000. The Japanese design architecture facilitated the production of tiered models (low, mid, and high-end) by adding features like freeze-frame and slow motion. In contrast, the complex V-2000 was inherently expensive to produce, even in its base configuration. Philips' initial failure to offer a feature-rich model—despite the V-2000's technical aptitude for still and slow-motion playback—formed a significant strategic error.

Philips filed an anti-dumping complaint with the European Commission. To underscore the gravity of the situation, President Wisse Dekker threatened to relocate production to low-wage regions if the pricing disparity was not addressed. Fearing trade barriers, Japanese manufacturers agreed to voluntary import restrictions.

However, the V-2000's decline was irreversible, primarily due to the emergence of the pre-recorded video cassette market. Film studios, acknowledging the permanence of VCR technology, collaborated on content distribution. Rental and copying firms favored VHS and Betamax due to the larger installed user base and the reliability of the hardware used for duplication. The V-2000's high breakdown rate required duplicators to maintain expensive reserve stock, an investment they declined to make.

The scarcity of pre-recorded media proved decisive, as 85% of usage involved viewing rental content. The V-2000's primary differentiator—extensive programming capability—was undervalued by consumers compared to content availability and cost. Marketing personnel identified this structural weakness shortly after launch; video rental inventories in Eindhoven typically stocked children's titles for the V-2000, but lacked major motion pictures or adult content. Although the video division formulated plans to negotiate with distributors, executive leadership failed to execute decisive action.

In late 1983, Philips publicly conceded the commercial failure of the V-2000, pivoting to a "multi-systems approach" that incorporated the sale of VHS recorders. Despite internal consensus regarding the proprietary system's terminal status, the firm publicly denied plans to abandon the V-2000. This contradictory stance was met with widespread skepticism from the press, retailers, and the general public.

Manufacturing operations transitioned to VHS production. During the 1984 annual report presentation, Vice President Cor van der Klugt disclosed the cessation of V-2000 production, while noting that substantial inventory remained to satisfy residual demand. This disclosure proved strategically erroneous. Retailers, already wary, interpreted the statement as a definitive termination signal and ceased procurement. To stimulate liquidity, Philips was compelled to implement drastic price reductions. The formal discontinuation of the V-2000 was announced in February 1986, more than thirty months after the internal decision to pivot.

General Motors (Based on Case II-5: "General Motors Corporation: The Downsizing Decision" in *"The Strategy Process"*, Quinn et al. (1988) and *"The Change Masters: corporate entrepreneurs at work"*, Kanter (1983): 320–324)

IN SEARCH OF THE CORE OF CORE COMPETENCIES

By the late 1960s, US public sentiment had shifted, reflecting growing concern over automotive pollution. Legislative action followed in the form of Clean Air Act Amendments, which mandated stricter emission standards. To achieve compliance, General Motors developed the catalytic converter, scheduled for production in late 1974 to meet the 1975 regulatory deadline.

Simultaneously, the industry faced the dual challenges of rising foreign imports and projected fuel cost escalation. Imports, predominantly small vehicles, targeted a segment largely ignored by American manufacturers, whose design philosophy favored size. Import market share grew from under 5% in 1962 to over 10% in 1968, with projections in 1969 anticipating a rise to 14% by 1970.

In 1970, General Motors convened an internal Energy Task Force. Its 1972 findings concluded that: (1) an energy crisis was imminent; (2) a federal strategic response was absent; and (3) energy costs would materially impact GM's operations, necessitating independent mitigation strategies. The 1973 oil embargo validated these concerns, inflicting severe negative consequences on the firm. Consequently, GM resolved to produce smaller vehicles aligned with fuel efficiency mandates, environmental standards, and shifting consumer preferences.

GM's history with the compact segment was problematic. From 1965, the firm battled negative publicity regarding the Corvair, famously critiqued in Ralph Nader's *Unsafe at Any Speed* following a fatal accident attributed to design flaws. Despite praise for its innovative design, the Corvair's rear suspension system became the focal point of a national scandal, leading to its discontinuation in 1969. The Vega, introduced in 1970, similarly failed; it suffered from higher-than-expected pricing and severe quality deficits, including engine overheating, chassis corrosion, and safety liabilities.

Following the sales collapse triggered by the oil embargo, GM identified the need for a sub-compact model (the Chevette) and a smaller luxury vehicle (the Cadillac Seville). Concurrently, a fleet-wide weight reduction initiative was launched to enhance fuel efficiency, with the initial reduction target of 400 pounds rapidly escalated to 1,000 pounds.

The Chevette required an accelerated concept-to-market cycle of 18 months—an unprecedented speed for GM. To achieve this, the firm implemented novel methodologies: the establishment of a cross-divisional central Project Centre (integrating engineers from Pontiac, Oldsmobile, Buick, Chevrolet, and Cadillac) and the leveraging of international competence, specifically Opel's small-car expertise. The global 'T car' platform—designed in Germany, manufactured in Brazil, and refined in England—served as the Chevette's foundation, enabling adherence to the aggressive deadline.

Subsequent models underwent progressive downsizing and mass reduction. Skeptics predicted market failure given the entrenched American preference for large vehicles, particularly as fuel prices stabilized. However, consumer reception was unexpectedly positive, as the vehicles maintained perceived spaciousness. As one executive noted, 'I said the only difference the customer would notice was that he had more room to walk around it in his garage' (Quinn et al. 1988:447).

Following the Chevette's successful 1975 launch, production was cut by 50% the subsequent year as falling gas prices spurred a faster-than-anticipated return to larger vehicles. GM also faced competitive pressure from Ford, whose "Welcome to the home of the Whopper" campaign highlighted its shift to producing the largest cars in the US. Undeterred, GM persisted with downsizing, introducing the 'X-body'—a front-wheel-drive platform half a ton lighter than its predecessors with comparable interior volume—and developing a mini car alongside further fleet-wide reductions.

GM's performance appeared robust until 1979, when sales contracted from $66 billion to $58 billion due to import competition, high interest rates, and global recession. despite profitability initiatives, revenue erosion continued through 1981 and 1982, forcing the US auto industry to acknowledge the structural cost advantage of Japanese imports.

While the subsequent 'I car' and 'A car' platforms outperformed the 'X-body', persistent quality issues afflicted GM vehicles. The 'J car' suffered from cold-start failures and sluggish acceleration, earning comparisons to the Edsel (Ford's model-based failure). regarding recalls—a proxy for quality control—GM ranked second only to Subaru between 1978 and 1982.

1978 – 1982: % of Sales Recalled

Brand	%
Subaru	97%
General Motors	86%
Chrysler	47%
Ford	45%
Volkswagen	38%
Honda	35%
Nissan	20%
Toyota	20%

Van Gelder Papier (Based on a case taught by drs. C. Luscuere for the course "Lijn B", Doctoraal II, Semester I, 1989/1990, as described in the corresponding course book)

In the 18th century, Pieter Schmidt van Gelder, the proprietor of a paper mill, sought to preempt succession disputes among his four sons. To ensure an equitable inheritance, he acquired additional mills, allocating one to each heir. This arrangement proved commercially viable, eventually consolidating into a regional paper monopoly.

Following the Second World War, the corporate entity was formally structured. Headquartered in Amsterdam, the firm operated five geographically dispersed factories across the Netherlands: Velzen (strategically situated for raw material import), two in Renkum, one in Apeldoorn, and one in Wapenveld. The firm's primary output was newsprint, facing limited competition from smaller entities such as KNPF in Maastricht.

Strategic success was based on high aggregate demand, monopolistic dominance, and institutional protectionism. Demand consistently exceeded supply, creating a backlog of orders and rendering marketing superfluous. Consequently, the Amsterdam headquarters functioned primarily as a procurement hub, leveraging monopsony power to negotiate favorable pricing for wood and cellulose. Labor relations were characterized by dependency and compliance; the lack of alternative employment in the sector ensured workforce stability despite low wages. Furthermore, the Ministry of Economic Affairs enforced protectionist tariffs to insulate Van Gelder from lower-priced foreign competition.

Central management maintained a laissez-faire relationship with the production units. Factory managers exercised significant operational autonomy, driven by the singular objective of volume maximization. Since sales capacity was constrained only by production output, the factories formed the critical locus of value creation, resulting in heterogeneous organizational structures across locations.

In 1966, the firm posted a minor deficit, which management dismissed as anomalous. However, as losses escalated in 1967, the Supervisory Board—comprising influential business leaders—intervened. Diagnosing the issue as a management deficit, they appointed an external professional: an accountant from Thomassen Drijver Verblifa, a firm with a comparable centralized structure. His mandate was to centralize control and integrate the autonomous factories. He implemented accounting-based control mechanisms to standardize operations and eliminate redundancies. However, the incumbent Amsterdam management, unfamiliar with these methodologies and excluded from the consultation process, viewed him with skepticism and withheld support. Simultaneously, the factories resisted the loss of autonomy by manipulating reporting data. Consequently, the initiative failed, and the manager departed on medical leave within nine months.

Losses intensified in 1968, yet management remained inert, prioritizing administrative trivia such as the accountant's severance package. Following a transient recovery in 1969, losses mounted again in 1970, prompting the resignation of several directors. The Supervisory Board intervened a second time, recruiting a manager from KBB with a dual mandate: restore profitability through rigorous control or, failing that, secretly pursue a strategic alliance with KNP.

The trajectory of the 1970s was predetermined by a pivotal event in 1955. Van Gelder was offered exclusive Dutch rights to a US patent for coated paper, a critical input for the magazine industry. Management rejected the offer based on skepticism regarding the magazine market's potential and a "not-invented-here" bias, arguing they would have developed the technology internally were it significant. Competitor KNP subsequently acquired the patent, leveraging it as the foundation for its future growth.

By 1970, the magazine market had expanded robustly, exceeding KNP's production capacity. Having ceded market leadership, Van Gelder sought to acquire KNP to restore its dominance. However, the KBB manager's focus on secretive negotiations diverted attention from Van Gelder's operational turnaround.

Throughout the negotiations, Van Gelder's strategic leverage eroded, allowing KNP to emerge as the dominant party. After nine months, a proposal materialized wherein KNP would acquire Van Gelder. Despite the unfavorable terms, Van Gelder lacked alternatives. When the Supervisory Board narrowly voted to disclose the plan to the second management echelon (factory directors), the reaction was hostile. The second echelon threatened to obstruct the integration, forcing corporate management to abort the merger, leaving Van Gelder in an unstable position.

As losses escalated in 1971, ABN Bank (the primary lender) installed a commissioner as Chairman of the Supervisory Board. Concluding that independent survival was impossible and domestic consolidation untenable due to internal resistance, he sought a foreign partner. Within six weeks, a majority stake (51%) was sold to Crown-Zellerbach (US). This initiated an 'Americanization' of management, re-attempting standardization and control systems. However, factory non-compliance persisted, and losses continued.

McKinsey was retained to advise on restructuring, recommending the closure of Apeldoorn and the divestiture of Wapenveld in 1974. The factories countered with viable alternative business plans based on an assessment of internal competencies. Consequently, the drastic measures were postponed, the local plans were implemented, and the American management team, having failed to revitalize the firm, repatriated.

By 1977, the firm faced critical insolvency and petitioned for government subsidization. The Ministry of Economic Affairs mandated an external audit by an independent party, explicitly excluding management consultancies. This assessment was subsequently executed by the Netherlands Investment Bank (NIB). Adopting a bottom-up analytical framework—in contrast to McKinsey's methodology—the investigator characterized the firm not as a cohesive entity, but as a fragmented collection of autonomous units ('islands'). Management reasoned that acknowledging this fragmentation offered a solution: the systematic dismantling of factory-level autonomy. The investigator was subsequently appointed to the corporate management team but engaged directly with the production units instead of breaking down factory autonomy. Factory leadership cooperated with the NIB investigator, formulating new strategic plans grounded in pre-existing, local innovation initiatives. However, the Supervisory Board expressed consternation that the new director had deviated from its directives. Consequently, the director was terminated, and McKinsey was re-engaged.

In 1979, McKinsey recommended a final intervention strategy: 'relative autonomization', effectively granting independence to all factories. While this precipitated a marginal recovery, it proved untimely. ABN Bank withdrew support and petitioned for bankruptcy in 1980. Following the formal declaration of bankruptcy in 1981, a 'Phoenix effect' ensued: the factories executed buy-outs from the estate. Viable operations were reformed, leading to a period of prosperity for the independent units.

Concurrently, an asbestos facility in Wormer was shuttered due to environmental hazards and the infeasibility of adaptive reuse. Despite the closure, the workforce maintained a rigid behavioral routine, returning daily to the vacant facility to socialize (play cards), while adhering to traditional break schedules. This persisted until demolition rendered the site inaccessible. The psychological impact was epitomized by graffiti left by a worker: *"bastards, why are you going bankrupt?"*

170

APPENDIX B

(Based on Ashby 1958:207-208)

The law is of general applicability, and by no means just a trivial outcome of the tabular form. To show that this is so, what is essentially the same theorem will be proved in the case when the variety is spread out in time and the fluctuation incessant…

Let D, R, and E be three variables, such that each is an information source, though "source" here is not to imply that they are acting independently. Without any regard for how they are related causally, a variety of entropies can be calculated, or measured empirically. There is H(D,R,E), the entropy of the vector that has the three components; there is H(E|D), the uncertainty in E when D's state is known; there is H(R|D,E), the uncertainty in R when both E and D are known; and so on.

The condition […] that no element shall occur twice in a column, here corresponds to the condition that if R is fixed, or given, the entropy of E (corresponding to that of the outcome) is not to be less than that of D, i.e.

$$H(E) \geq H(D).$$

Now whatever the causal or other relations between D, R and E, algebraic necessity requires that their entropies must be related so that

$$H(D) + H\_D(R) = H(R) + H\_R(D),$$

for each side of the equation equals H(R,D). Substitute H(E) for H(D), and we get

$$H(E) + H\_D(R) \leq H(R) + H\_R(E) \leq H(R,E).$$

But always, by algebraic necessity,

$$H(R,E) \leq H(R) + H(E) \quad H(E) + H\_D(R) \leq H(R) + H(E)$$

i.e.

$$H(E) \geq H(D) + H\_D(R) - H(R)$$

Thus the entropy of the E's has a certain minimum. If this minimum is to be affected by a relation between the D- and R-resources, it can be made least when $H_D(R) = 0$, i.e. when R is a determinate function of D. When this is so, then H(E)'s minimum is H(D) - H(R), a deduction similar to that of the previous section. It says simply that the minimal value of E's entropy can be forced down below that of D only by an equal increase in that of R.

E = outcome, R = regulator, D = disturbance

APPENDIX C

As indicated, developing a specific organizational chart to manage core competencies is infeasible and contradicts the principle of minimum critical specification. However, I propose several processes or guidelines that form the minimal requirements for core competence management. These represent necessary conditions rather than guarantees of success. Drawing on the organizational principles detailed in Chapter 4 and the theories of Best and Porter, the following components of an infrastructure or strategic architecture (Prahalad & Hamel 1990) are identified.

1. Explicate core competencies Following an analysis of existing competencies and core competencies, findings must be disseminated throughout the firm. Organizational members must be sensitized to the significance of these competencies to enable them to conceptualize the implications for workflows and their individual roles. It must be emphasized that possessing core competencies is a baseline, not an end goal; a culture of continuous development must be cultivated. Sub-competencies should be targeted for maturation into core competencies. Consequently, a clear assessment of the current state and future potential of core competencies is required. New competencies must be identified, and specific objectives established to elevate existing competencies to the status of core competencies.

A critical component of explication is prioritization. All core competencies are vital, and performance evaluation must reflect this. Members must understand that the organizational focus has shifted to their specific contributions to core competencies, which will serve as the primary basis for performance assessment.

2. Establish core competence networks within the organization Project groups centered on core competencies should be established. Participation must be voluntary and spontaneous rather than mandated by management. Leadership within these groups should be determined by the participants themselves via election. To incentivize engagement, the organization may consider granting special status to participants.

The primary objective of these groups is information exchange. This facilitates the comparison of routines, the transfer of knowledge and experience, and the exploration of the competencies' potential. This exploration includes clarifying and transferring competencies, improving them, identifying novel applications, analyzing market developments, and defining the conditions necessary for exploitation.

Inter-competence project groups may be formed to examine potential combinations or to identify gaps in knowledge and capabilities across the organization. Such collaboration can be guided by managerial directives emphasizing that the recombination of core competence components may give rise to new core competencies.

These groups foster frequent information exchange, enabling members to understand and potentially operate within other fields of expertise. This enhances both learning potential and organizational flexibility. Universal access to information is a prerequisite for this process.

Management is responsible for facilitating these groups by providing necessary infrastructure, such as databases, electronic communication tools, and dedicated time and space for unimpeded participation. Management must also make complementary investments in resources shared across all competence groups. Furthermore, management must establish frameworks for evaluating members. Assessment should focus on participation, willingness to share information, and contributions to core competencies. Peer evaluation is essential, as participants are best positioned to assess these metrics. Conversely, management should evaluate the aggregate performance of the group. This structure incentivizes critical peer monitoring, as underperformance by individuals negatively impacts the group's overall results. Robust methodologies must be developed to ensure effective evaluation.

Groups must possess the decision-making and executive authority to implement their conclusions and proposed actions. However, they must compete for resources at the management level. Management allocates resources (capital and expertise) based on the assessed improvement potential of the core competencies. This competitive allocation mechanism motivates groups to strive for continuous improvement to secure necessary resources.

3. Institutionalize Customer Value A focus on Customer Value is fostered by exposing every organizational member to its delivery. Routines directly related to Customer Value must be embedded in the repertoires of all members, ensuring continuous exposure to its importance and a clearer understanding of the organizational whole. This focus is reinforced by developing specific variables for evaluating Customer Value, such as time, quality, environmental impact, or cost. This adds a dimensional constraint—for example, delivering value with minimal lead time, minimal environmental impact, or lowest cost. This contextualizes Customer Value, establishing a framework for performance evaluation and heightening awareness of its criticality.

Furthermore, management must emphasize the importance of satisfying the needs of emerging trends and early adopters. This involves encouraging novel and unconventional approaches to the delivery of Customer Value.

4. Stimulate an entrepreneurial attitude An entrepreneurial mindset is critical for continuous improvement. A primary inhibitor of entrepreneurship is organizational intolerance for error. Consequently, the organization must cultivate a climate that accepts failure and the unsuccessful implementation of new ideas. Indeed, early failure should be welcomed as a mechanism for rapid feedback. Since error generation is a prerequisite for learning—a process vital to core competence development—mistakes should be positively reinforced rather than penalized.

Organizational members are responsible for adaptive learning and implementing corrective actions when deviations occur. Concurrently, generative learning requires collaboration between staff and management. While this is primarily an individual responsibility, management should provide support and stimulation (e.g., the scenario method at Shell; de Geus 1988). Accountability should focus on participation in adaptive and generative learning processes, rather than on penalizing errors, which serve as necessary conditions for learning.

Performance evaluation and reward systems must integrate the generation of new ideas. To encourage this, all improvements, regardless of scale, should be visibly attributed to the originator, thereby motivating the broader workforce. New ideas should never be summarily discarded, even if they diverge from prevailing paradigms, as every idea possesses potential value.

Innovation can be further stimulated by establishing rigorous standards for technology, usability, quality, and reliability. Methodologies such as job enlargement, job enrichment, and job rotation are also effective. Peters (1991, p.11) advocates for a horizontal career path rather than the traditional vertical trajectory, where promotion involves lateral movement toward different core competencies.

5. Create openness with the environment Firms focused on core competencies require a high degree of environmental openness to capture external influences. Strategies to increase environmental exposure include selecting highly competitive suppliers who introduce cutting-edge products, thereby forcing the firm to adapt and innovate. Similarly, serving demanding customers and early adopters compels the firm to concentrate on product improvement. Furthermore, maintaining intensive relationships with knowledge centers is essential; these hubs generate research that the firm can leverage to improve and expand its core competencies.

Additionally, the firm must maintain a continuous search for qualified talent, independent of immediate vacancies. This ensures acquiring unique capabilities and signals quality to the labor market, attracting further talent. Finally, the firm must continuously study existing, new, and unconventional market actors (customers, suppliers, competitors) to rapidly identify and respond to emerging developments.

6. Introduce pluralism into the organization Pluralism is vital for core competence-oriented firms, as it enhances the diversity of insights required for problem-solving, environmental responsiveness, and learning. This pluralism must permeate all levels, from management to staff. To reinforce the customer perspective beyond the institutionalization of Customer Value (see point 3), the organization might integrate external mechanisms, such as a customer council comprising independent individuals who may or may not be current customers.

7. Upgrade the resources Beyond financial capital, a firm's primary resources are its human capital. It is required that employees individually acquire knowledge and experience; thus, internal and external training require significant attention. The application of this new knowledge must be encouraged and rewarded. Resource upgrading is also achieved through internal standards, such as horizontal promotion, where employees must cycle through all core competencies before reaching executive management. This ensures management possesses comprehensive competence knowledge. Senior managers may even engage in new core competencies without this being perceived as a demotion. Viewing employees as permanent resources justifies the investment in training and capability acquisition. While the risk of turnover exists, it should not deter investment in the firm's most critical asset. Furthermore, treating employees as permanent fosters loyalty.

A definitive method for upgrading resources is through their allocation. Core competencies must compete internally for resources. Management is responsible for allocating resources to those competencies demonstrating the highest potential for improvement. This allocation strategy ensures that resources are deployed where they can be utilized most effectively, thereby maximizing their upgrade potential.

8. Avoid imposing structures A firm's self-organizing capacity is essential for flexibly managing environmental change and variety. Consequently, management must refrain from interfering with how organizational members structure and organize their activities; this responsibility resides with the members. Efficiency concerns also fall within their purview. Given the context established by the preceding points, members possess a holistic overview and are competent to address these issues. Furthermore, due to their specific expertise, they may be better positioned than management to resolve such matters.

Cybernetic theory suggests that it is preferable for management to define constraints (undesired states) rather than to prescribe specific objectives and the plans to achieve them. By identifying what to avoid, management empowers members to determine the path toward desired outcomes. This does not imply managerial passivity; intervention is warranted when processes deviate from viable trajectories. However, the guiding principle is intervention rather than prescription. Management should identify deviations, engage in dialogue with members, establish conditions for problem resolution, and permit the members themselves to generate solutions.

These eight guidelines synthesize the holographic organizing principles with the components of core competence. Customer Value is institutionalized, while the Knowledge Base is continuously expanded through resource upgrading, entrepreneurship, learning processes, and pluralism. Managerial Capabilities are primarily focused on creating conditions, providing support, and avoiding structural imposition. Redundancy is embedded in the repertoires of organizational members through networks, the institutionalization of Customer Value, environmental openness, and pluralism. The requisite variety dimension is defined by the immediate environmental conditions faced by organizational members, implying that openness to the environment must be preserved where it is directly relevant. Minimum critical specification is reflected in the avoidance of imposed structures, the self-development of networks, and the explicit articulation of core competencies. Finally, the learning to learn dimension is expressed through the entrepreneurial attitude, environmental openness, pluralism, and resource upgrading. It is emphasized that these guidelines represent the minimal conditions for creating an environment conducive to core competence management. They are not guarantees of success; rather, they must be subjected to critical analysis and double-loop learning to ensure continuous refinement.

APPENDIX D

This case study examines the Nedlloyd transport conglomerate. The analysis commences with a descriptive overview of the firm's development from its inception in 1970 through 1988, outlining the emergence of its various operational activities. For the period post-1988, a granular examination of each activity is provided to trace specific developmental trajectories. The following historical reconstruction relies on Oosterwijk (1988), annual reports spanning 1977–1991, and archival articles from the Financieel Dagblad.

Nedlloyd Group N.V. was formed through the consolidation of Stoomvaart Maatschappij Nederland (SMN), Koninklijke Rotterdamse Lloyd (KRL), Verenigde Nederlandsche Scheepvaartmaatschappij (VNS), and Koninklijke Java-China Paketvaart Lijnen (KJC-PL)—the latter having previously acquired Koninklijke Paketvaart Maatschappij (KPM) in 1967. This merger was formalized on January 20, 1970, under the corporate entity Nederlandsche Scheepvaart Unie (NSU). In late 1977, NSU was rebranded as the Nedlloyd Group, and in 1981, the conglomerate further expanded by absorbing the Koninklijke Nederlandsche Stoomboot-Maatschappij (NSM).

The primary operational focus of the core firms was liner shipping, which subsequently became the conglomerate's strategic pillar. The merger was precipitated by the ascent of major foreign shipping consortia, the dissolution of traditional operational boundaries attributable to containerization, and the potential for efficiency gains through the rationalization of liner services. Consequently, the objective was to rationalize the core liner operations and establish international partnerships to expand the network. Complementing these liner services, the group maintained operations in bulk cargo (dry bulk, oil, LPG, etc.).

At the time of the merger, KRL and SMN held profitable stakes in non-maritime activities, including stevedoring, shipping agency and forwarding services, air freight, and tourism; these assets were retained. By 1972, forwarding and international road transport emerged as significant growth markets. Although the travel and tourism sectors underperformed, the firm continued to invest, notably through equity participation in Martinair and North Sea Ferries.

Bulk services operated within a volatile market characterized by substantial overcapacity following the oil crisis. Liner shipping was similarly impacted by the oil shock and the ensuing economic recession. In 1974, Nedlloyd (then operating as NSU) strategically diversified into the global energy sector, specifically oil and gas exploitation, through the establishment of Neddrill. The rationale for this entry was twofold: to hedge against escalating fuel prices—a critical cost driver for the firm—and to capitalize on a growth market, particularly in third-party oil and gas extraction.

Nedlloyd underwent periodic restructuring. In 1976, all international transport and forwarding entities were consolidated under Damco International Transport. By 1977, the firm adopted a dual-pillar structure: the Maritime Group and Other Activities. The Maritime Group comprised four divisions: Nedlloyd Lines, Nedlloyd Bulk, Neddrill, and Nedlloyd Shipping Services. The Other Activities pillar included the Ports Division, Specialized Transport, Damco, and the Industrial Services Division. Following the 1981 acquisition of KNSM, two additional divisions—Transavia and Mammoet Transport—were integrated.

Divisional performance during the 1982–1983 period was mixed. Neddrill, Bulk and Tanker Shipping, and Nedlloyd Lines posted poor to disappointing results, whereas Mammoet Transport, Specialized Transport, Damco, and Transavia performed reasonably well. In 1984, Nedlloyd initiated the decentralization of Nedlloyd Lines to enhance flexibility and customer orientation through streamlined communication. The division was segmented into smaller units, each with independent profit responsibility. While performance improved by 1985, the extent to which this was attributable to decentralization remains ambiguous, given the concurrent economic recovery, increased transport volumes, and the appreciation of the dollar.

In 1985, organizational flexibility and responsiveness were prioritized as strategic objectives, formalized in Project "Koers" (Course). This initiative aimed to enhance the quality of external and internal services through intensified inter-unit cooperation. Although the board claimed to observe early positive outcomes, these were neither specified nor substantiated in subsequent reporting. Concurrently, the firm signaled the diminishing strategic centrality of traditional maritime shipping, redirecting substantial investment toward Other Transport and Energy, with the latter viewed as particularly critical.

Despite the Energy division sustaining heavy losses in 1986, corporate commitment to the sector persisted. Strategic objectives included mitigating oil price dependency and aligning with logistical trends. Nedlloyd aspired to evolve into a 'total transport concern', integrated across all ways (maritime, terrestrial, and aerial). To this end, the firm acquired Van Gend en Loos (VGL) from NS—anticipating the European Single Market of 1992—and Netherlines (aviation) to capture the growing regional air transport market.

1987 served as a year of consolidation with minimal structural alteration. Investments were directed toward Transavia and the Energy division. Furthermore, as part of the ongoing integration process, the logistical capabilities of various subsidiaries were aggregated into Nedlloyd Districentres.

By the conclusion of 1987, Nedlloyd had transitioned from a strictly maritime entity to a comprehensive transport conglomerate. Beyond liner services and bulk transport, the firm had established a presence in land and air transport, while retaining a strategic emphasis on the energy sector. The overarching objective was to develop into an integrated total transporter, augmented by energy interests.

In 1988, Nedlloyd's board was destabilized by the intervention of Norwegian investor Torstein Hagen, who asserted a significant equity stake (approximately 24%). Hagen proposed the consolidation of several European shipping firms into a single entity, 'Eurolines', with Nedlloyd as the nucleus. His strategy advocated an exclusive focus on the core activity of maritime shipping, specifically containerization. Hagen argued that only through such integration could European firms compete effectively with global giants such as Evergreen (Taiwan), Maersk Line (Denmark), and P&O (England). This hostile maneuvering precipitated contentious shareholder meetings, the implementation of protective anti-takeover measures, and, critically, a strategic reassessment. To retain control, the board was compelled to articulate a compelling counter-strategy and vision to secure shareholder support.

To align corporate strategy with Torstein Hagen's proposals, the 1987 annual report sought to delineate Nedlloyd's future portfolio with greater precision. Within the emergent paradigm of "logistical services," three primary activities were defined: global container logistics anchored by proprietary shipping routes, a European-scale distribution network, and specialized transport with at least a European scope. Concurrently, the Energy division was retained as a mechanism for risk diversification.

In the 1988 annual report, the board adopted more formal management nomenclature, designating these logistical operations as "core activities," while classifying energy operations as "strategic interests." Subsequently, the strategic emphasis on energy diminished; by the following year, "strategic interests" were downgraded to mere "interests." Likely responding to renewed pressure in 1990 from Hagen—who advocated for a strict focus on maritime and land transport—Nedlloyd designated its aviation assets for divestiture. Similarly, Energy and Neddrill were marketed for sale, contingent upon valuation. Consequently, the Energy division was sold, and all equity in Transavia was transferred to KLM in two phases.

The following section profiles specific Nedlloyd divisions from 1988 to 1991.

Container Logistics This division manages a global logistical network via liner services, operating both independently and through partnerships. Container volume demonstrated consistent growth, with the exception of 1991, when a more selective cargo acceptance policy precipitated a decline. Operating results improved through 1989, contracted sharply in 1990, and subsequently recovered. The 1990 downturn was attributed to the Gulf crisis and adverse market conditions—specifically the depreciation of the US dollar—despite an increase in transported volume.

Beginning in 1989, Nedlloyd implemented a mainstream/feeder concept to aggregate cargo flows and optimize service density. Concurrently, the firm developed Ultimate Container Carriers (UCC), vessels distinguished by high capacity. To enhance customer orientation, an integrated service suite branded as the 'Flowmasters' package was introduced. However, references to the 'Flowmasters' initiative cease in the 1990/1991 reporting period.

Bulk Shipping: This division specializes in the maritime transport of dry and liquid bulk commodities. While transported volume and revenue exhibited volatility, operating results generally trended upward, with the exception of 1991, where revenue growth coincided with declining results. The fleet comprises vessels specialized for dry bulk (5), chemicals (5), and petroleum products (3). From 1990, several vessels were transferred to joint ventures to leverage economies of scale.

Mammoet Transport: Mammoet Transport focuses on the global logistics of project cargo and heavy/oversized freight via land and sea. Financial performance was negative starting in 1987 but showed a positive trajectory, achieving profitability in 1989 and continuing to improve thereafter. In 1989, the division merged with the German entity Hansa-Linie.

Nedlloyd Road Cargo: Established in 1989, this division encompasses European road and rail groupage, partial-load services, container trucking, international liquid/chemical transport, air freight forwarding, and general services. Revenue was volatile, and financial results were negative. Underperformance was attributed to the high costs of integrating core firms and intense competitive pressure on freight rates.

Districentres: Upon its establishment in 1987, Nedlloyd Districentres reportedly achieved immediate positive outcomes. The division provides comprehensive third-party inventory management, including storage, assembly, packaging, invoicing, customs clearance, distribution, and contract warehousing. However, the financial picture is ambiguous. While revenue demonstrated a sharp upward trend—notably achieving 30% organic growth in 1991—operating results remained negative.

Division Van Gend & Loos (VGL): VGL operates a high-density distribution network within the Benelux region, handling general cargo ranging from small parcels to palletized shipments via express and 24-hour services. Since 1987, the division has posted continuous growth in transport volume and revenue. Profitability also improved consistently throughout this period, plateauing only in 1990.

Faxion: Faxion functions as an international partnership specializing in garment-on-hanger distribution. Nedlloyd expanded this division through acquisitions and joint ventures across various countries. Revenue and volume are highly correlated with climatic conditions affecting apparel sales, leading to significant fluctuation and negative results in 1991. Strategically, the portfolio was diversified to include value-added services such as inventory management, labeling, cleaning, and order processing.

Refrigerated/Frozen: This unit manages the transport and distribution of refrigerated and frozen cargo (cold chain logistics). despite initial operational challenges, efficiency improvements and revenue growth enabled the division to achieve profitability for the first time in 1991, following a period of progressively decreasing losses.

ECT: In 1988, a merger was announced involving Nedlloyd's "Quick Dispatch" stevedoring unit, Rotterdam-based Müller-Thompsen, and Europe Container Terminus, forming Europe Combined Terminals (ECT). Operations encompass the handling of containers, automobiles, and fruit, alongside bonded warehousing, distribution, and conventional break-bulk cargo. Financial results were initially positive but turned negative in 1991. Nedlloyd's 44% equity stake in ECT is designated for potential divestiture.

BIBLIOGRAPHY

Abell D.F. & J.S. Hammond (1988), "Portfolio analysis" in *The strategy process* Quinn, Mintzberg and James, Prentice-Hall International Editions, pp.597-602

Abernathy W.J. & K. Wayne (1974), "Limits of the learning curve" in *Harvard Business Review*, sept/oct.

Ansoff I. (1987), *Corporate Strategy*, Penguin Business Books, Londen Argyris C. (1977), "Double loop learning in organizations" in *Harvard Business Review*, sept./oct., pp.115-125

Ashby W.R. (1958), *An Introduction to cybernetics*, Chapman & Hall Ltd., Londen

Best M.H. (1990), *The new competition: institutions of industrial restructuring*, Polity Press, Cambridge

Boston Consulting Group GmbH & Partner (1992), "Kommentare: Vorstand und Vision (VIII): Fähigkeiten und Positionen", München

Braun von C.F. (1990), "The acceleration trap" in *Sloan Management Review*, herfst, pp.49-58

Braun von C.F. (1991), "The acceleration trap in the real world" in *Sloan Management Review*, summer, pp.43-52

Bryans P. & T.P. Cronin (1983), *Organization Theory*, Core Business Studies, Mitchell Beazley Publishers, Londen

Cool K. & D. Schendel (1988), "Performance differences among strategic group members" in *Strategic Management Journal*, Vol.9, pp.207-224

Dankbaar B., J. Groenewegen & H. Schenk (1990), *Perspectives in Industrial Organization*, Kluwer Academic Publishers, Dordrecht

Dankbaar B., J. Groenewegen & H. Schenk (1990), "Recent economic developments and the prospects of industrial organization" in Dankbaar et al (eds) (1990), *Perspectives in Industrial Organization*

Diericks I & Cool K. (1989), "Asset stock accumulation and sustainability of competitive advantage" in *Management Science*, Vol.35, dec., pp.1504-1511

Dinklo J.A. (1992), "De toekomst van een onderneming", Bottom Line Conferentie, 17 November, Eindhoven

Dongen van E. (1993), "Business units, soelaas of helaas? Onthullingen over unit management" in *Bedrijfskundige Berichten*, March, pp.7-9

Dosi G. (1984), *Technical Change and Industrial Transformation*, The Macmillan Press Ltd., Londen

Freeman C. (1990), *The economics of innovation*, Aldershot

Geus de E.P. (1988), "Planning as learning" in *Harvard Business Review*, March/April, pp.70-74

Gluck F., S. Kaufman & Walleck (1982), "The four phases of strategic management" in *The Journal of Business Strategy*, Vol.2, Jan., pp.9-21

Harrison E.F. (1987), *The Managerial Decision-Making Process*, 3rd edition, Houghton Mifflin Company, Boston

Haspeslagh P. (1982), "Portfolio planning: uses and limits" in *Harvard Business Review*, Jan/Feb.

Henderson B.D. (1979), *Henderson on corporate strategy*, Abt Books, Cambridge, 3rd print

Henzler H. (1988), "Von der strategischen Planung zur strategischen Führung: Versuch eine Positionsbestimmung" in *ZfB*, pp.1286-1307

Hill C.T. & J.M. Utterback (1979), *Technological Innovation for a Dynamic Economy*, Pergamon Policy Studies-50

Itami H. with Roehl (1987), *Mobilizing invisible assets*, Harvard University Press, Cambridge, Massachusetts

Jarillo J.C. (1988), "On strategic networks" in *Strategic Management Journal*, Vol.9, pp.31-41

Leonard-Barton D. (1992), "Core capabilities and core rigidities: a paradox in managing new product development" in *Strategic Management Journal*, Vol.13, pp.111-125

Mansfield E. (1968), *Industrial Research and Technological Innovation: An Econometric Analysis*, Longmans, Green & Co Ltd., Londen

Marshall A. (1938), *Principles of economics*, 8th edition, Macmillan and Co., Londen

Metze M. (1991), *Kortsluiting: hoe Philips zijn talenten verspilde*, SUN Nijmegen

Mills D.Q. & B. Friesen (1992), "The learning organization" in *European Management Journal*, Vol.10, No.2, June 1992

Morgan G. (1983a), "Rethinking Corporate Strategy: A Cybernetic Perspective" in *Human Relations*, Vol.36, pp.345-360

Morgan G. (1983b), "Action Learning: A Holographic Metaphor for Guiding Social Change" in *Human Relations*, Vol.37, pp.1-28

Morgan G. (1986), *Images of Organization*

Nelson R. & S. Winter (1982), *An evolutionary Theory of economic Change*, 10th print, Harvard University Press, Cambridge, Massachusetts

Penrose E.T. (1972), *The theory of the growth of the firm*, Oxford, Basil Blackwell, 5th print

Peters T. (1991), "Get innovative or get dead: Part Two" in *California Management Review*, winter, pp.9-23

Pile S. (1979), *The book of heroic failures*, Futura Publications, Londen

Polanyi M. (1983), *The tacit dimension*, Gloucester, Massachusetts

Porter M.E. (1980), *Competitive strategy*, The Free Press, New York

Porter M.E. (1985), *Competitive Advantage*, The Free Press, New York

Porter M.E. (1990), *The competitive advantage of nations*, The Macmillan Press Ltd, Londen

Porter M.E. (1991), "Towards a dynamic theory of strategy" in *Strategic Management Journal*, Vol.12, pp.95-117

Prahalad C.K. & G. Hamel (1990), "The core competence of the corporation" in *Harvard Business Review*, May/June, pp.79-91

Quinn J.B., H. Mintzberg & R.M. James (1988), *The Strategy Process: concepts, contexts, and cases*, 10th print, Prentice-Hall International Editions

Rumelt R.P. (1982), "Diversification strategy and profitability" in *Strategic Management Journal*, Vol.3, pp.359-369

Schumpeter J.A. (1987), *Capitalism, socialism and democracy*, 6th edition, Counterpoint Unwin Paperbacks, Londen

Seeger J.A. (1988), "Reversing the images of BCG's growth/share matrix" in *The strategy process* in Quinn et al (1988), pp.602-605

Senge P.M. (1990), "The leader's new work: building learning organizations" in *Sloan Management Review*, fall, pp.7-23

Stalk G., P. Evans & L.E. Shulman (1992), "Competing on capabilities: the new rules of corporate strategy" in *Harvard Business Review*, Jan./Feb., pp.57-69

Steers R.M., G.R. Ungson & R.T. Mowday (1985), *Managing effective organizations*, Kent Publishing Company, Boston, Massachusetts

Teece D.J. (1982), "Towards an economic theory of the multiproduct firm" in *Journal of economic behaviour and organization*, pp.39-63

Teece D.J. (1986), "Profiting from technological innovation: implications for integration, collaboration, licensing and public policy" in *Research Policy*, 15, pp.285-305

Teece D.J. (1988), "Technological change and the nature of the firm" in Freeman (1990), *The economics of innovation*

Teece D.J., G. Pisano and A. Shuen (1990), "Firm capabilities, resources, and the concept of strategy", CCC Working Paper 90-8, Center for Research on Management, University of California, Berkeley

Williams J.R. (1992), "How sustainable is your competitive advantage?" in *California Management Review*, lente, pp.29-51

Williamson O.E. (1975), *Markets and Hierarchies: analysis and antitrust implications*, The Free Press, Londen

Winter S. (1988), "Survival, Selection, and Inheritance in Evolutionary Theories of Organization" in Singh (ed) (1990) *Organizational Evolution: New Directions*, Sage Publications, Newbury Park

Zucker L.G. (1977), "The role of institutionalization in cultural persistence" in *American Sociological Review*, Vol.42, pp.726-743